THE

Well-Read

LIFE

"*The Well-Read Life* is not just a book about reading more or reading better. It is an invitation, richly laden with quotations from the classics, to what Dorothy Day called 'the revolution of the heart,' one good book at a time. Anyone who takes up Marcie and Colleen's invitation to a 'well-read life' already glimpses the beauty of this story-driven revolution. I say: join them!"

Catherine Cavadini
Author of *Saints: A Family Story*
Director of the Master of Arts Program in Theology
University of Notre Dame

"Why should we read? How do we make time to read good books in a busy world? And how do we read well to transform our hearts, minds, and communities? Marcie Stokman and Colleen Hutt answer these questions and more in this resource for all readers and aspiring readers. Full of the wisdom of great authors of the past and present, this book will motivate you to 'take up and read.'"

Haley Stewart
Author of *The Grace of Enough* and *Jane Austen's Genius Guide to Life*

"Well-Read Mom is a gift. These women are truly changing culture from the home outward, and this book invites more readers to join them in their work. With so many touching stories shared from the writers' own experiences, reminders from great literature, quotes from saints and heroes of the past, and plenty of tangible action steps to follow, this book is the first book you should read once you remember how necessary reading is for the beautiful life you crave."

Jessica Hooten Wilson
Fletcher Jones Endowed Chair of Great Books
Pepperdine University

THE
WELL-READ
LIFE

Nourish Your *Soul*
through Deep Reading and
Intentional Friendship

MARCIE STOKMAN
COLLEEN HUTT

AVE MARIA PRESS AVE Notre Dame, Indiana

© 2024 by Marcie Stokman and Colleen Hutt

All rights reserved. No part of this book may be used or reproduced in any manner whatsoever, except in the case of reprints in the context of reviews, without written permission from Ave Maria Press®, Inc., P.O. Box 428, Notre Dame, IN 46556, 1-800-282-1865.

Founded in 1865, Ave Maria Press is a ministry of the United States Province of Holy Cross.

www.avemariapress.com

Paperback: ISBN-13 978-1-64680-320-0

E-book: ISBN-13 978-1-64680-321-7

Cover image © Fotograf / AdobeStock.

Text design by Esther Moody.

Printed and bound in the United States of America.

Library of Congress Cataloging-in-Publication Data is available.

To Pete, thank you for being my companion, my roots, and my ally. Thank you for your quiet strength and practical wisdom. It is a joy to be on this journey together. "Oh, magnify the LORD with me, and let us exalt his name together!" (Ps 34:3).

—MS

To Colin, thank you for asking me to be your life's companion. You help me to stay in front of what is most essential—loving God and loving people.

To my children, Dominic, Cecilia, Justin, Sophia, and Peter, who have fueled my imagination, provided numerous and necessary occasions for me to grow in humility and tenderness, and made my search for meaning come alive with greater intensity and urgency.

—CH

A story is a way to say something that can't
be said any other way, and it takes every word
in the story to say what the meaning is.
—Flannery O'Connor, *Mystery and Manners*

Brothers, do not be afraid of man's sin, love man also
in his sin, for this likeness of God's love is the height
of love on earth. Love all God's creation, both the
whole of it and every grain of sand. Love every leaf,
every ray of God's light. Love animals, love plants,
love each thing. If you love each thing, you will
perceive the mystery of God in things. Once you have
perceived it, you will begin tirelessly to perceive more
and more of it each day. And you will come at last to
love the whole world with an entire, universal love.
—Fyodor Dostoevsky, *The Brothers Karamazov*

Contents

Why I

QUIT READING...

and How I Started Again

> "Time doesn't stop. Your life doesn't stop and
> wait until you get ready to start living it."
> —Wendell Berry, *Hannah Coulter*

When did I (Marcie) stop reading? It wasn't like one day I devoured literature, and the next day I didn't. It didn't happen that way. But it did happen. Slowly, over a few years, and without much of a fight, I quit reading quality literature.

Not that I stopped reading altogether. I perused articles. I tackled books on parenting, Christian living, and homeschooling. I studied work-related journals, self-help books, and much more. What fell by the wayside was the leisurely reading of literature for my own personal enjoyment and growth.

I was post-college, married, mothering, working, and managing a household. Life was getting busier, and something had to give. Reading for pleasure seemed to be a luxury I couldn't afford.

"Is reading for pleasure even necessary?" I wondered.

It might not have been a conscious thought, but an attitude of efficiency was creeping into my thinking. I told myself that reading a novel in the midst of a full and busy life squandered time and energy I did not have. Before I knew it, sitting down with a hefty novel or even a short one felt not only unnecessary but, even worse, a waste of time.

Then one day, this point of view was challenged by a friend who invited me to join her book club. For the next ten years we worked our way through the classics, reading books that challenged and stretched us. Some selections were ancient classics; some were long and complex. My time away from books had taken a toll on my mental powers: Sometimes I wrestled with a paragraph trying to comprehend what I was reading. Often, I wasn't able to finish a selection, or I didn't remember details from the books when I did finish.

And yet, I had to agree with my friend when she said to me, "I live better when I'm in the pages of these kinds of books." Month after month I trudged along, many times only finishing several chapters of the month's selection. I would prop a book up in front of my kitchen faucet so I could ponder a paragraph while washing dishes. My motto became *Read what you can in the time you have.*

I left guilt behind. My limits didn't seem to matter. Even the attempt to read and discuss these kinds of books was helping my life. As I pondered the literature, my everyday life became more interesting and engaging. Looking back, I see that reading literature was leading me to wonder about one of life's most pressing questions: *What does it mean to live well—and how can I begin to live that way myself?*

I was beginning to understand that "living well" had something to do with cultivating a rich interior life: to grow, question, understand, wonder, and connect with others. It involves thinking deeply about ideas and situations, recognizing beauty, and being hushed by awe. These experiences happen again and again when I read and discuss great and worthy books with others. It entails living with wonder, in order to be fully alive. Wonder is a springboard for life-changing questions and conversations.

This sense of wonder—combined with slow and careful reading, or "deep reading," as I later came to call it—produced in me a kind of inquisitiveness that drew me into intentional friendships with others who were asking these same questions and craved these kinds of conversations. Souls who, like me, wanted a well-read life.

RECOVERING FROM DISTRACTION

So, what happened at the end of those ten years with the book club? Why are those women in the original club not still part of my life?

Well . . .

Because we moved to a new city.

Because Pete and I had small children.

Because our family grew, and life picked up speed.

Because. Because. Because.

Soon I found myself surviving, not thriving.

Looking back, I see that almost everything I needed to do for my family took precedence over nurturing my own soul. I didn't fight to take care of my mind and my heart. Why not? Why was investing in my own "living well" not a priority? How could I so easily and without much of a second thought allow this meaningful experience to vanish without objection?

Perhaps you know the answer to this. Perhaps my experience is not so different from yours.

Maybe you are a woman who read voraciously in high school and college. You loved it, but now, with the demands of being a mom, precious little time exists for reading literature. You want to get back to it, and you keep telling yourself you will, but it will have to be some time in the future. It can't be now. You need a break at the end of the day, after all, and the lure of screens tempts you away from the demands of the printed page.

Maybe you're a woman who sits in front of a computer all day long, and the last thing you're interested in after work is more sitting, especially with a challenging Russian novel in your hands. I get it.

Maybe you got by in school without cracking a book and reading it from cover to cover. Instead, you skimmed and leaned heavily on YouTube clips, summaries, and SparkNotes to fill the gaps. You even scored As in your literature classes! It happens.

But now, for some reason, you find yourself wanting to get away from the screens, to slow down and focus. Maybe a gnawing suspicion is nudging you. "Something's been missing in my life. I want more than shallow surfing, enticing influencers, and an endless to-do list."

Now you have *this* book in your hands. You intuit that reading and discussing literature could open the door to the deeper meaning and friendship you long for. Perhaps you glimpse a possibility for you to return to enjoying literature or become an intentional reader for the first time.

You can! You will. That is what this book is about. A journey to becoming well read awaits, and so do the rewards.

BEGINNING AGAIN

I started this introduction by explaining how I quit reading. This is how I began to read again.

One day in 2012, my daughter Bethany, then a new mom, called me nearly in tears. "Mom, I'm not going back to that mothers' group. I've been there three times, and all they talk about is their kids and what kind of diapers to buy. Mom, isn't there a place after college where women get together and talk about the real questions in life?"

Ouch! I heard a cry of loneliness and longing in her voice, and I hurt. A mom hurts when one of her kids hurts. What was really going on with Beth? She was tuning in to her deeper desire to live well. She was waking up to her longing for more—more connection, more meaning, more conversation, more friendship.

At this time, I was giving a series of talks to mothers of preschoolers in northern Minnesota, where I live. I titled this series "Well-Read Mom." Even though I wasn't reading literature regularly, I was curious to learn about these mothers' reading practices. Looking back on it now, I think I was also trying to resurrect my own reading practices.

Each time I gave my talk, I found myself driving home sad. Why? Because most of the women were not reading . . . anything. The number one reason they gave was "I don't have time."

Not one woman was reading quality literature for her own enjoyment. I realized I was struggling, too. All of us could agree that reading is important, yet it wasn't happening in our lives.

My talk only served to make the women feel guilty. It's like I was saying, "Hi, I'm here to point out one more way you're failing as a mom. You're not doing enough. You're not reading enough. And you're not smart enough." This was not my intention! I wanted to encourage the women—and myself—to enjoy reading, but the little talk I was giving was not helping anyone take a step to read more, share life more, and live in wonder.

So, when Beth called that day and I heard that cry of loneliness in her voice, something happened. Her desire to take care of her heart through meaningful conversation and friendship merged with my desire to read more and read well, and just like that, Well-Read Mom was born.

AN IDEA TAKES HOLD

The idea was simple. We would read great and worthy books together. She would gather a group of friends in St. Paul, and I would do the same in Crosby. By reading the same book during the same month, we would stay together and hold each other accountable in our reading.

It started that simple, and interest grew. By the end of the first year, there were twenty-five women leading groups and following along with us. This was clearly meeting a need for connection, meaning, and friendship, and women were responding. Beth was not the only one with a cry of the heart. It is a human cry.

Since Well-Read Mom began, we have witnessed thousands of women (and men) find a way—in the midst of busy lives—to read more and read well. Still, there are those who hesitate and are leery of joining in. Often, we hear comments like "I think reading is important, but I just don't have the time," which often masks a deeper or hidden concern that is more difficult to verbalize: "What if I can't comprehend these kinds of books? What if I can't keep up? Is literature even relevant today?"

We want to shout, "Yes, it is!" First we will show you why we need to read literature, and then we will show you how to read it. This book is about awakening your desire to read. You deserve to become well read, not only for your own growth and happiness but for your children, your family, and our society. Technology is changing our society's very definition of what it means to read. This book is about moving forward by taking a step back—to the basics.

We will look at reading. What does it have to do with your humanity and growth in holiness? How can you improve your reading ability, comprehension, and focus? It is possible, and it starts with awakening desire. Maybe joining a book club doesn't fit in your life right now (or maybe it does). Either way, by following along in this book, you will be on your way to reading and enjoying literature, whether it's a habit renewed, or a practice begun.

Either way, it all begins with a first step. This book is that step.

GETTING STARTED

There are three "big ideas" that are shaping how we write this book:

1. *To have a "well-read life" means first recognizing, then overcoming, certain obstacles that arise all around us.* Cataclysmic cultural changes are sweeping across our world, changes that affect not only what we read but also *how* we read. To cultivate a well-read life is to recognize these obstacles and take a step against this mind-numbing cultural tide.

2. *To reap the benefits of a well-read life, we must feed our mind well, engaging what we read intentionally and actively.* Together we will work to understand how deep reading strengthens our minds, enhances our critical-thinking ability, and improves our ability to focus. We will acquire the skills necessary to retrain the brain, reversing the effects of the daily use of technology.

3. *We draw closer to the Lord, and to one another, as we grow in our humanity.* By reading this book, you will begin to recognize the connection between reading literature and growing in empathy, humanity, and faith. Enriching our souls in this way is not a small thing. You will read stories of personal transformation from readers across the country. You will understand how a quote or a particular section from a book can convey timeless messages and eternal truths that impact and bring about change in a woman's life.

Why become a better reader, or cultivate a well-read life? Reading literature is about raising our awareness of what it is to be a human being. We read deeply not for information but for transformation and wisdom. Jessica Hooten Wilson said it best: "We read not to turn our minds off but to turn our hearts on."[1] Our hope is that by the end of this book, you will experience transformation in your life, too.

Strengthen your mind. Enrich your soul.

PART ONE

Reading the Culture

"You don't have to burn books to destroy a
culture. Just get people to stop reading them."
—Ray Bradbury, *Fahrenheit 451*

We have a problem: the way we read has changed. As more and more people put down books and pick up screens, there is a shift from pleasure reading to potentially mindless scrolling. Why is this a problem? Digitization has reshaped reading, which in turn has changed the way we think. We desire to look for goodness, truth, and beauty in the world, but our minds are caught in an endless barrage of information that keeps us from slowing down and thinking deeply. Reading great and worthy books is one way to feed our minds and souls with goodness, truth, and beauty.

CHAPTER 1

The Way We
Read
Is Changing

"There is some good in this world,
and it's worth fighting for."
—J. R. R. Tolkien

*N*ot long ago I (Marcie) was in a little café, writing an article. The waitress eyed my stack of books on the table curiously. "Do you mind if I ask what you do?"

"Oh, I help run a national book club for women."

"Gosh, I can't even remember the last time I read a book," she commented as she refilled my coffee cup. "In fact, I bet it's been . . . I don't know, eight years since I've even held a book."

Reaching in her pocket, she held up her phone, "But I don't need to. I've got this, and it's all I can do to keep up with my social media. It is plenty of reading, believe me." When she left, I felt sad for her. Yes, she is reading, maybe more than ever, throughout the day and even into the night, but she's missing out on another kind of reading. And the worst part is, she doesn't know that she is missing out. And the waitress is not alone. Many young people and many adults today find themselves with all the reading they can keep up with on their phones and laptops.

In 2007, when Apple introduced the iPhone with its bells, whistles, and full internet capacity, the definition of phones changed forever. So did our long-standing definition of what it means to read.

Innumerable subtle and not-so-subtle changes followed, including two monumental changes that can easily be overlooked: *how* we read (on devices), and *what it means* to read (scanning and scrolling for information). Both these changes represent a cataclysmic shift.

In her book *How We Read Now,* Naomi S. Baron brings this evolving perception to light: "Since online technology is tailor-made for searching for information rather than analyzing complex ideas, might the meaning of 'reading' become finding information rather than contemplating and understanding?"[1] Technology is changing our society's very notion of what it means to read. What used to be taken for granted—that reading literature and other books is a way to grow in understanding and depth of knowledge—is progressively being forgotten as digital reading becomes dominant.

It is worthwhile to distinguish between two kinds of reading: digital and deep.

DIGITAL READING

Since smartphones are increasingly deemed necessary to navigate through life, most of us are already doing all the scanning, scrolling, responding, and digital reading we can manage. This becomes problematic when another kind of reading, the kind we experience when we are lost in the pages of a book, gets pushed aside.

Reading through the medium of a device changes the way we read because there are a multitude of distractions built into the platform itself. Advertisements pop up, notifications get sent, reminders ding, hyperlinks proliferate across the page (leading one down a variety of rabbit holes). All these things take us away from our initial purpose—to focus on the words on the page and to be carried to where the author wishes us to go.

Reading on screens defeats us before we even begin for one simple reason: the medium *itself* encourages this continuous, partial attention. The Canadian philosopher Marshall McLuhan famously captured this idea in his book *Understanding Media* when he coined the phrase "The medium is the message." McLuhan continues, "The 'message' of any medium or technology is the change of scale or pace or pattern that it introduces into human affairs."[2]

The "change of scale or pace or pattern" new technologies introduce into our lives must be thoughtfully considered and their net effects managed if we are to stop this unsettling decline in the ability to think, reason, and imagine. While scanning devices is a relatively new phenomenon, it has drastically changed the way we read in an alarmingly short time frame. In ten years, we went from reading predominantly in print to absorbing information primarily on screens. This change, from print to digital, has affected both what (content) and how (method) we read.

Remember the days of sitting down and reading the newspaper in its entirety? According to a recent *Slate* article, when people read digitally, the majority tend to finish less than 50 percent of an article (whereas 80 percent of people are likely to read a printed article to the end).[3] With digital text, we tend to skim and multitask because of the way information is structured for the screen. We tend to see the process not as something to enjoy for its own sake but as something to "get through" before we click the next thing.

THE PHYSIOLOGY OF READING

Intuitively, we know that settling in with *Pride and Prejudice* is much different from skimming a Facebook post. What we may not realize is that too much digital reading can make "deep reading" of literature and other printed matter more difficult, because it changes how we read. So, if you are finding it harder now to focus on a printed book, there may be good reasons for that.

For example, studies show that the digital layout of a screen has changed our eye patterns. Web developers and programmers have developed digital layouts to train the brain to absorb information more efficiently, on a neurobiological level. Words are formatted differently on the screen. Here are some of the most common gaze patterns programmers use when designing content on the screen: heat map, F-pattern, Z-pattern, "layer-cake" pattern, spotted pattern, marking pattern, bypassing pattern, commitment pattern, and so on.[4]

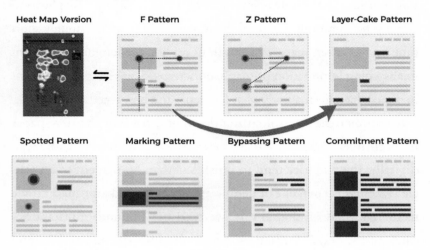

With digital reading, our eyes skim the screen in these patterns, but when we read from a book, our eyes move in a linear pattern from left to right. Why is our eye pattern different when reading on a screen? In part because advertisers want to direct our focus to ensure we see the advertisements they are peddling. Eye patterns are designed to promote partial attention. With a barrage of information coming at us, we often don't make an informed judgment about what is being advertised but instead react with an impulse to consume. Consumeristic reading does not engage the brain as slow, focused attention does.

In addition to the advertising agenda embedded in digital reading, there is a nearly insurmountable volume of content available. In his 1981 book *Critical Path*, futurist R. Buckminster Fuller estimated that until 1900 human knowledge doubled every century, but by 1982 human knowledge was doubling every twelve to thirteen months.[5] Now we are on our way to doubling knowledge *every twelve hours*.[6] With so much coming at us, we triage and process as quickly as we are able.

Faced with such a tsunami of information, our brains are forced to adapt quickly in order to manage the unmanageable, figuring out what to pay attention to and what to disregard. And this discernment must happen fast! We search for keywords to grasp the text's context and draw conclusions. Rapid-fire decision-making is part of the digital experience.

We begin to assume that scrolling headlines, scanning news bites, and tapping screens is reading—and it is. But it is not reading for meaning. There is another kind of reading, which fosters the opposite experience of hurrying—one that cultivates and fosters a slowing-down relaxation, a filling-up restoration, and a making space for contemplative thought. This is the kind of reading we don't want to miss out on. It is called *deep reading*. If we don't use our deep-reading brain, we risk losing or not developing the complex circuitry needed for a deep-reading experience.

DISCOVER DEEP READING

The term *deep reading* was first coined by Sven Birkerts in *The Gutenberg Elegies* (1994), where he described it as "the slow and meditative possession of a book. We don't just read the words; we dream our lives in their vicinity."[7]

This kind of reading—the kind in which we "dream our lives"—is far more likely to occur as we savor the pages of good literature than when we rapidly scan a screen to get the gist of a movie review, for example. It involves slowing down, and even stopping at times, to ponder a phrase or revisit a paragraph a second or third time. It involves receiving a story and allowing ourselves to follow where the author is taking us—as this reader recently discovered.

Stories of a Well-Read Life
The Anticipated Pleasure of Reading

One day last fall, I sat down with *Charis in the World of Wonders* by Marly Youman. Summer had been full of activities: company, kids, travel, and grandchildren. So, in September, I read this book in the early morning, in the evening, and sometimes in the afternoon for whatever time I had. I experienced staying with this novel—all the way through.

It took a couple of chapters to get into the story, but when I did, I understood what had been missing in the busy days of company: the pleasure of reading. Reading for no other reason than to enjoy it and discuss it with friends.

One morning as I unloaded the dishwasher, I felt a flush of anticipation and wondered, "What is it that I am looking forward to today?" Suddenly, I knew I could go back to that story. I was experiencing restorative leisure, the kind that comes through losing oneself in the pages of a book and is a surprisingly pleasurable experience.—MS

When we deliberately slow our reading pace, specific cognitive processes are engaged. We recollect, imagine, reflect, analyze, infer, and contemplate. And engaging in these cognitive processes fosters increased empathy, critical thinking, self-reflection, relaxation, restoration, and enjoyment. We are helped to develop the habits of paying attention. Where digital reading cultivates a habit of continuous, partial attention, deep reading cultivates disciplined, focused attention. This skill enhances our quality of life.

Entering the zone of deep reading is an entirely different experience. Rather than fragmenting our attention, it focuses it. And this fully focused attention builds thoughtful awareness that transfers to thoughtful listening and conversation skills.

WHAT ABOUT AUDIOBOOKS?

When we are first making room in our lives for literature, the temptation can be strong to rely on audiobooks or other "shortcuts" to accomplish reading goals more quickly (such as finishing a book before our next group meeting!). However, those who are trying to "retrain the brain" in order to process what they are reading more thoughtfully may want to consider the benefits of the physical act of reading words on a page.

Our friend Shannon discovered the dangers of multitasking. While listening to an audio recording of *Brideshead Revisited*, she folded laundry on her kitchen table, took meat out of the freezer for dinner, and answered the doorbell before throwing another load in the washing machine. As she responded to an incoming text message on her phone, she found herself irritated by the audio. "I had no idea what was going on in this story," she admitted, "and finally, I shut it off."

To Shannon's credit, rather than give up on the experience, she found her book, sat down on the back steps, and began reading with focused attention. "It was a completely different experience," she told me. "It was restorative!"

Audiobooks have their place, but if our time spent listening (or reading) lacks focused attention, we will soon discover how much we are missing. Remember, the goal is not to multitask but to be refreshed and to discover. We need to garner the skill of managing our attention.

READING TO CONNECT WITH THOSE WHO HAVE GONE BEFORE US

When I (Marcie) was a new mom, there was one book in particular that helped me navigate through some lonely days: Dorothy Day's *The Long Loneliness*. In this autobiography, she shares a simple incident involving her neighbor Mrs. Barrett, a stay-at-home mom in her New York neighborhood whose daughter, Kathryn, was Dorothy's playmate.

> It was Mrs. Barrett who gave me my first impulse towards Catholicism. It was around ten o'clock in the morning that I went up to Kathryn's to call for her to come out and play. In the front bedroom, Mrs. Barrett was on her knees, saying her prayers. She turned to tell me that

Kathryn and the children had all gone to the store and went on with her praying, and I felt a warm burst of love toward Mrs. Barrett that I have never forgotten, a feeling of gratitude and happiness that still warms my heart when I remember her. She had God, and there was beauty and joy in her life. All through my life what she was doing remained with me. Mrs. Barrett in her sordid little tenement flat finished her breakfast dishes at ten o'clock in the morning and got down on her knees and prayed to God.[8]

As I read, I made a connection with Mrs. Barrett, an ordinary mom, doing her duty and seeking her God. What Mrs. Barrett didn't know was that her faithful, ordinary work and prayer would have something to do with the conversion of a modern-day saint. The little girl at the door became Servant of God Dorothy Day. Nearly a hundred years later, both Mrs. Barrett and Dorothy Day became an inspiration in my life.

I was a new mom, living in a new city, struggling through a great deal of change and trying to come to grips with the responsibilities that come with a newborn. I was lonely. I felt my life at home with an infant lacked meaning. I didn't know anyone in the neighborhood, and I'd look out my apartment window, hoping to see someone outside I could go talk with. Little Jim was fussy, and I couldn't seem to calm him down. Lonely, isolated, and confused, I felt inadequate as a mother.

It was at this juncture in life that we visited my husband's parents. Eyeing *The Long Loneliness* on my mother-in-law's bookshelf, I pulled it down. I was struck by the title. Though I had no idea who Dorothy Day was, I knew something about loneliness. Bringing the book back to our apartment, I remember being awed by the simple story of Mrs. Barrett as she knelt in her kitchen.

I had never knelt to pray in my kitchen; I was trying to learn to clean it at the time. But like Dorothy Day, I experienced "a burst of love" for Mrs. Barrett as she, hidden in her home, hung up her dish towel and said her prayers. That day, after tackling my kitchen, I knelt and cried out to God. "Lord," I pleaded, "I don't like being a mother. I don't feel good at it. I know it is important work, but it doesn't feel like it. I didn't think motherhood would be so lonely. Please teach me how to live this."

Dorothy Day was moved by Mrs. Barrett. I was, too. Reading about her seemingly insignificant gesture brought about a change in me. Thank you, Mrs. Barrett; hidden away in your tenement flat, you sought God. And thank you, Dorothy Day. Your story found me during the hidden years of motherhood and helped me seek God in such a way that my loneliness was transformed into longing.

READING THAT SPARKS US INTO ACTION

Not only does deep reading profoundly change the way our brain functions, it also changes our hearts. As a friend once said, "The spark that kindles the imagination in one person can catch fire in another."

That's what was happening to me as I read *The Long Loneliness*. What caught fire was a desire to love God as Dorothy Day and Mrs. Barrett did—in hidden ways. And this desire rose in me through the pages of a book.

A few years (and a few kids) later, there was a knock on my back door. It was Joe Plutt, a retired professor from my parish. When I answered, he handed me *Sorrow Built a Bridge* by Katherine Burton. While cleaning out his library of books, he came across this biography of Rose Hawthorne and thought I might enjoy it. Already in the middle of six or seven books at the time, I did what I thought prudent: dropped everything and read the book straight through.

I was fascinated. Not only was Rose the daughter of the great American author Nathaniel Hawthorne, but she was also a convert to Catholicism and, even more extraordinary, she was on her way to becoming a canonized saint. Imagine my surprise when I was reading *All Is Grace: A Biography of Dorothy Day*, and discovered that Day also read *Sorrow Built a Bridge* and it was this work that inspired her to start the Catholic Worker movement.

The capacity of books to spark a fire in us, to move us to action and bolster courage, was confirmed once again. Passing on the flame through reading and sharing great and worthy books impacts us and has the potential to impact our culture too. *Culture building* happens through changed hearts. Mind to mind and heart to heart, our imaginations are awakened and desires are sparked that can and will move us to action.

Stories of a Well-Read Life
A Monk Helps a Mom

"Mom, I can't study in our house," my teenage daughter informed me. "It's too messy. I need to go to the coffee shop."

"Really? You can't find a place to study here?" But I glanced across the house and realized that Emma was right. Scattered papers lined the counter and miscellaneous items were scattered everywhere.

At that time, I was reading Thomas Merton's *The Seven Storey Mountain*. In Merton's autobiography, I became aware of his obedience to his superiors. Even in the little, seemingly insignificant and mundane monastery tasks, obedience mattered.

As I read, my eyes were opened. Was I running from my vocation? It is easy for me to avoid the little tasks of homemaking thinking, "Surely this banal work of sorting this and organizing that isn't important." But I was coming to realize, obedience in the little things would bring more order, and increased order would bring greater calm to our home. Maybe then all of us could study and think and enjoy our life together in the house.

I wouldn't have thought that reading a biography of a monk in a monastery would help me with my own vocation, but it did. Again and again, reading literature connects me to meaning in my days and helps me live my vocation with intentionality. In *The Reed of God*, Caryll Houselander writes,

> There are many people in the world who cultivate a curious state which they call "the spiritual life." . . . The only time that they do not regard as wasted is the time they can devote to pious exercises. . . .
>
> All the time spent in earning a living, cleaning the home, caring for the children, . . . cooking, and all the other manifold duties and responsibilities, is regarded as wasted.
>
> Yet it is really through ordinary human life and the things of every hour of every day that union with God comes about.[9]

When reading literature is part of our ordinary life, it brings us into the deeper realities and mysteries of life. What good is a treasure like St. Augustine's *Confessions* or Emily Brontë's *Jane Eyre* if we never find the time to work our way through it with focused attention? We won't be able to receive the treasure. In

order to experience the transforming wisdom available to us,
deep reading and time are essential.—MS

WHY READ? WHY WRITE?
TWO SIDES OF THE SAME COIN

Reading presupposes writing. Nothing can be read that is not
first written. Pause with me (Colleen) for a moment and consider
how both reading and writing have been at the service of culture
through human history.

Writing began in Mesopotamia around three thousand years ago
with the invention of cuneiform: sign becoming synonymous with
sound. Cuneiform marks the first known writing in the history
of civilization. This idea spread west to the Nile and east to the
Iranian Plateau and eventually to Egypt and Greece. Every culture
that encountered this new way of immortalizing sound changed
the concept and "alphabet" to fit their own needs.

Writing, and the interpretation of those signs as "reading," en-
abled commerce; it provided a system of communication across
distances and a means of preserving culture. Writing (and thus
reading) became a permanent testament to what was most essential for a people. Once writing became standard (by making permanent the sounds of the human voice and creating a common
symbol to communicate them), we could capture and memorialize
any moment in time. The Sumerian *Epic of Gilgamesh* (2100 BC)
is the oldest written story known to exist; its preservation allowed
generations afterward to have a window into this period of time.

> "Choose to live and choose to love;
> choose to rise above and give back
> what you yourself were given."
> —*Epic of Gilgamesh*[10]

In the Beginning: Storytelling as an Oral Tradition

The first stage of human communication actually predates writing, when stories were told and retold orally. The ancient Greeks thought literature was best encountered through hearing rather than by reading, because it could be experienced viscerally and in the context of community. We can think here of the Greek tragedies and comedies being performed on stage to educate the citizenry about their cultural values.

In the fall of 2020, just weeks before the presidential election between Joe Biden and Donald Trump, our book group was reading Sophocles's tragedy *Antigone*. One of the issues this play explores is how to treat a political enemy. Our discussion did not change which candidate we endorsed, but it made us think about how we would treat those of differing views on the day after the election. We left the meeting with a greater desire for dialogue and the restoration of civility in our society. If we seek to humiliate our political enemies after a victory, something essential to society will be lost as well, which is a valuable lesson to meditate on in the midst of an election year.

Stage Two: Writing to Organize and Preserve

The change from telling stories orally to writing them down was a major shift in culture that allowed such epics as Homer's *Iliad* and

Odyssey to be preserved, beginning the collection of what would be known as the "Western Canon." It is amazing that we would know nothing of the dialogues of Socrates, the founder of the Western philosophical tradition, without Plato, who had the foresight to write these conversations down.

Plato and Aristotle gave us the basic parameters of education, or the "liberal arts," consisting of the study of grammar, logic, and rhetoric, and secondarily arithmetic, geometry, music, and astronomy. Later in the Middle Ages, these became ratified as the "Trivium" (grammar, logic, and rhetoric) and the "Quadrivium" (arithmetic, music, geometry, and astronomy). *Trivium* means "where three roads meet," and the study of grammar, logic, and rhetoric were understood to operate more like concentric circles—going deeper in the understanding of reality—than as a linear progression of one subject to the next.

Aristotle's *Organon* attempts to categorize language and determine how language communicates truth. What Aristotle means by *grammar* is an encompassing conversation, but for our purposes here it means not only the "nuts and bolts" of language—such as defining *verb*, *noun*, *subject*, and *predicate*—but also seeing how these ideas are embodied in reality. Grammar is understanding the basic facts in each subject area, the "how, what, where, and when." Grammar gives us "the knowledge of particulars."[11] It is the building block of knowledge that eventually leads a person to question why something is the way that it is. The "why" is taken up in the study of logic. And rhetoric is the ability to communicate and to persuade using logic. Rhetoric is a blending of science and art—knowledge of things (truth) and eloquence.

Stage 3: Reading to Grasp, Persuade, and Reveal Truth

In the study of logic, we move from understanding particular things to abstract thinking. Through logic and dialectic, we can grasp the universal *in the particular*; we come to the "art of universals."[12] We deepen our ability to think critically. In the study of rhetoric, we learn how to synthesize what we have learned. We learn how to present knowledge to persuade, convince, or reveal what we have come to know. Why is this important?

From the beginning of Western civilization, it was understood that it was essential to learn how to read, how to think, and how to speak. Today, we are outsourcing our thinking to pundits and not taking the time to fill our souls with texts necessary for human flourishing. To learn the art of reading, thinking, and speaking is critical to maintain a free society. When we reduce our communication to incomplete fragments over texts or emojis, we are losing the capacity in us that makes us human.

Reading quality literature activates our brains and hearts. When we read, we are presented with a set of categories: words, action/plot, structure, and characters. We analyze, deduct, infer, and imagine why certain things happen in the story and not others. Through emotional connection with the characters, we see examples of how to live well or ill. We explore new dimensions of reality that are outside our particular place and time. In other words, we use the entirety of our mind, body, and soul to come to knowledge about ourselves and the world we live in. Literature shows us that a particular person who lived in a different moment of history, who had different religious beliefs or a different family structure, can nonetheless share something in common with contemporary people living today.

— *Stories of a Well-Read Life* —
Reading to Understand the World

When I read *Their Eyes Were Watching God* by Zora Neale Hurston, it was clear to me that the particulars of the life of the protagonist, Janie Mae Crawford, were very different from my own. Janie grew up in the South in the 1930s, a poor Black child who never knew her parents and was raised by her grandmother, Nanny. Life was a struggle and the opportunities for women were few and far between.

By contrast, I was raised in a loving, stable home by both my biological parents and given every opportunity for betterment. I never had to worry that my mother would marry me off after my first kiss for fear I'd become pregnant and bring shame upon the family. I never had to dread sharing my marriage bed with someone not of my choosing and whom I did not love. I never had to worry about being treated as an object rather than a person to be cherished.

And yet, even though the particulars of our lives looked quite different, I could see we shared certain longings: for community, for companionship, and for authentic love. Reading this book presented me with an opportunity to discover the "universal" desires that are found in the depths of every human heart. And having read it, I was reminded that what divides people (race, socioeconomic backgrounds, etc.) is not as important as our shared humanity. This book made the "knowledge of the universal" come alive to me.—CH

THE UNIVERSAL DESIRE TO KNOW (AND THE DANGERS OF UTILITY)

From the ancient Greeks through Christendom, the aim of education was knowing the transcendentals: unity, truth, goodness, and beauty. In a podcast episode entitled "Why the Liberal Arts Matter," Bishop Robert Barron acknowledged and lamented a recent decline in the study of liberal arts.[13] Barron says the liberal arts are the "free" arts (deriving from *liber* in Latin: "free"). These arts are "free from utility"—they are meant to be enjoyed for their own sake and therefore the knowledge they encompass is of a greater value to society than something studied for what it will produce.

The liberal arts, Barron claims, have to do with *meaning*. We can get the best job and make a wonderful living, but if we don't know *why* we are working, our work does not yield the joy it could. This is not to disparage the necessity of utility and the contributing factor of the high cost of college education, which has often forced students to choose majors based on economic benefits and repaying college debt. We all need a job, but our education should not be *reduced* to production. A "good job" does not equate with a happy life. We need to rediscover the true, the good, and the beautiful! These are what give meaning, value, and purpose to a human life. The transcendentals are the aim and end of the liberal arts. Knowledge of goodness, truth, and beauty is essential to being human.

Great literature, Barron claims, opens up "dimensions of the soul and meaning and purpose that you get nowhere else," because it addresses the values on which humanity is built. Therefore, when the liberal arts fade away, we are left with only utility. We are reminded of Mr. Gradgrind in Dickens's *Hard Times*: "Now, what I want is Facts. Teach these boys and girls nothing but facts. Facts alone are wanted in life. Plant nothing else and root out everything else . . . nothing else will ever be of any service to them."[14]

When knowledge is reduced to utility, we are in grave danger. We can know when this shift has happened in culture by reckoning when technology dominates a space once held by human endeavor. I am always amazed by the Apple commercial of a young child in a tent holding an iPad up to the sky, gazing at the screen as the stargazer app names the constellations he is looking at. Anecdotally, I've never seen a child use an iPad in that way. I *have* seen them play Candy Crush, Pokémon, or Fortnite until their eyes glaze over. When screens are constantly interrupting our ability to dwell in contemplation of the real things and offering us a tantalizing world of materialism (and "isms" of every sort), no wonder we are experiencing depression and anxiety at alarming rates.

> "We had the experience but missed the meaning, and approach to the meaning restores the experience in a different form, beyond any meaning we can assign to happiness."
>
> —T. S. Eliot. "The Dry Salvages"[15]

FINDING GOD "IN RAW NATURE"

Reading allows our mind to wonder, because it allows the work of our mind, heart, and imagination to be engaged. Professor John Senior, who cofounded the University of Kansas Integrated Humanities Program, witnessed the effects on students who were immersed in technology—whose lives included extended periods on TVs, computers, and other screens. He became convinced the way forward was to put students in front of what is "real." He wanted his students to experience stargazing, dancing, poetry, calligraphy, and large amounts of time spent in nature, because these pursuits often elicit wonder. In the essay "John Senior: Prophet of Tradition and Realism," Julian Kwasniewski writes, "For Senior, the mind had to be born in wonder if it was to be brought to wisdom, and this was only possible through experiencing God's creation 'raw.'"[16]

Stories of a Well-Read Life
Dante Outdoors

Dante's *Inferno* is a story that profoundly shaped my life when I read it in college. It helped me to realize that friends could lead me to God, that he sends the people we need as gifts to help us encounter him. It revealed to me that I didn't have to "climb" the mountain to God alone—in fact I should decidedly *not* do that—but rather follow the friends in my life and the friendships cultivated supernaturally with the saints, to come to know and love God.

Wanting to impart lessons like these to my fifteen-year-old son, I recently gave him his own copy of the book, and offered multiple times to begin reading the story with him. "Maybe later," he would say to me. Or, "Tomorrow tonight for sure." Yet tomorrow never came, and he continued to put me off. After extending multiple invitations, I decided to wait until he became curious about that book on his nightstand. And then one day, it happened.

"Mom, what do you say we start Dante now?"

I tried to contain my excitement. "YES! Sounds good! Bring your book downstairs!" Impulsively, I decided to re-create the opening of Dante's *Inferno*. Grabbing two camping chairs and a flashlight, I walked out the front door and down the road, over the bridge into the country road, my son trailing behind me.

"Where are we headed, Mom?" Peter wondered aloud.

I simply said, "You'll see."

THE WAY WE READ IS CHANGING | 23

We walked down the darkened road to a trail near our property. We continued until we were sufficiently nestled in the forest, listening to the eerie sounds of animals scampering through the trees and the wind creaking through the branches. There was not a light to be seen in any direction. I set the chairs down, turned on my flashlight, and began to read:

> Midway in the journey of our life
> I came to find myself in a dark wood,
> For the straight way was lost.[17]

I don't think either one of us will ever forget beginning Dante's *Inferno* that way. It was frightening. I said to Peter, "Imagine you have no idea where you are. You don't know that our house is just a quarter mile away and that you could make your way out of here. And as soon as you turn to walk, three snarling beasts stop you dead in your tracks. Sin can be like that—it's scary to be steeped in sin with no way out. That's why Dante was so grateful when a friend arrived to offer him a way out."

Re-creating the story as it is written from its setting in the dark wood brought a gravitas to these opening lines that will become part of our memory of Dante. Reading this poem in nature made it come alive.—CH

LIVING IN WONDER CHANGES US

Books also have a way of awakening wonder in us through characters who posit such enthusiasm for living. One morning, as my son, Peter, and I (Colleen) began our forty-five-minute commute to school, I noticed him, head down, staring at his phone. We live on a tiny island in Wisconsin, and we must cross a bridge to begin our drive into the city. This morning, the sun was glistening through the trees surrounding our island. The sun was a coral disk in the sky sending cascading patterns of colors across the lake, and several spectacular sandhill cranes were gliding above the waterline looking for their feast of frogs and insects.

The beauty of the moment overtook me, and I gushed (sounding alarmingly like the title character from L. M. Montgomery's *Anne of Green Gables*), "Peter, isn't it *positively lovely* that we live in a world with mornings like this one?"

Now, usually I do not speak like this! I would usually be more cerebral or interior about my revelations on beauty. But in reading *this* book, Anne's joie de vivre had infected me, and my natural tendencies gave way. Beauty became something that simply needed to be shared and delighted in. I could hear Anne in my mind saying to Matthew, "Isn't it a wonderful morning? The world looks like something God had just imagined for His own pleasure, doesn't it? Those trees look as if you could blow them away with a breath— pouf! I'm so glad I live in a world where there are white frosts, aren't you?"[18]

That morning in the car, something changed in the way we drive over the bridge each day. The bridge has become a reminder for Peter and me to find something to delight in about the nature surrounding us. *Anne of Green Gables* helped me to live differently. To be attentive to the needs we all have for friendship and to live in wonder of the world around us changes us for the better. There is a holy curiosity before reality that we cannot afford to lose. Deep reading is one way to open us up to that wonder.

Rather than spending our time scrolling trivialities and texting tweets, let's take up the challenge together to read great and worthy literature. As we do, we will be transported into the lives of heroines and villains, saints and sinners. Our imagination will be enlivened and shaped by role models to emulate and deceitful demons to avoid. By focusing on what is good and true and beautiful, a sense of wonder and a desire for greatness will be awakened.

Becoming well read involves an intentional commitment to a regular practice of deep reading. It doesn't matter where you are in your reading ability. What matters is your diligent commitment. If you persevere with us on this journey to become well read, our hope is not only that you will strengthen your deep-reading skills but that you will also come to increasingly recognize what St. Thomas Aquinas wrote to be true: "The slightest knowledge of the greatest things is greater than the greatest knowledge of the slightest things."

A WORK IN PROGRESS

Are you worried about your ability to experience the joy and benefits of deep reading? If so, you are not alone. The well-read life is a work in progress for all of us; it requires the kind of reading that may seem tedious and drawn out at times, especially if you're just beginning. A commitment is required. So is effort. But it is a worthy effort.

The purpose of this book is to encourage you to join in the journey of becoming well read. This laudable goal is easier to attain with a bit of camaraderie and accountability. Experience has shown us that to continue to read a work of literature in an attentive, life-changing way, we need each other—and a few essential tools that will help us get the most out of what we read. We will take a closer look at some of these in the next chapter.

ACTION STEPS

Part of reading well entails keeping a notebook or journal where you can record ideas, quotes, and other impressions. If you don't already have one, why not create one? Begin using your "reading journal" today by writing the title of this book on the inside front cover (for easy reference) and recording your responses to these questions as you read each chapter.

- Has your primary mode of reading changed from print to digital? What kinds of print and digital media do you use most often each day?
- What does it mean to you to be "well read"? Who are the well-read people in your life? Did their example play a part in your deciding to read this book?
- How have your family's digital habits changed over the last ten years? How has technology changed your relationship with printed materials?
- Write about the last time you experienced relaxation and restoration from your reading. What are some of the obstacles you experience in reading printed materials? What are some of the benefits?
- What steps can you commit to take from reading this chapter?

CHAPTER 2

The Way We
Relate to Others
Is Changing

"Man is essentially a story-telling animal, but
a teller of stories that aspire to truth."
—Alasdair MacIntyre, *After Virtue*

Are you thirsty for friendship, longing for someone with
whom you can share stories? Loneliness is real, and depending on social media is like drinking salt water—it only makes
us thirstier. On the other hand, women who read well often
benefit from being able to communicate more effectively,
having learned more about themselves and others from the
insights of authors, characters, and fellow readers. In the
midst of cultural changes and ideals, cultivating friendships
with like-minded people will help us to stand against toxic
influences and affirm and maintain a civil society.

Thirty-six years ago, when I (Marcie) was a new mom, Pete and
I moved to Omaha, Nebraska. We rented a little apartment, and

he started medical school. I was happy to be a mom, and yet (as I shared earlier) something was wrong. Really wrong. I was lonely, exhausted, and at my wits' end. My colicky infant son, Jim, screamed through the day, and he screamed through the night. And I didn't have one friend to share life with.

Later that year, Pete and I had a chance to serve on a mission trip in Guatemala. One day, I looked out the window of our little house and saw a group of Mayan women in their brightly woven skirts with baskets of laundry on their heads and babies strapped on their backs. They were heading to the lake. I was curious, so I followed them.

Standing up to their knees in the water with their children splashing alongside, the women scrubbed their clothes on the rocks. They talked and laughed. They shared life: they were friends. Watching from a distance, I had a moment of profound realization: "Something has been missing in my life, and now I know what it is. It's a community. I have a different kind of poverty. I have a washing machine and many opportunities, but I have a poverty of communal life."

My life has changed since then, but for many Americans the problem of isolation and loneliness has not gone away.

CULTURAL ISOLATION

In the 1950s, the influence of America's social, religious, service, and political institutions and organizations was at its peak. Church attendance was robust; men were being turned away from seminaries that were bursting at the seams. Civic and social institutions enjoyed strong, vibrant membership and participation. Social and fraternal groups like women's clubs, the Elks, and the Rotary Club were part of the fabric of every town. Veterans returning from World War II joined communities, got married, had babies, and participated in religious and civic life to a much greater extent than we do today. While there were many things America still had to confront—civil rights being among the most urgent—there was a collective sense of community, volunteerism, and the importance of religion.

In 2000, social scientist Robert Putnam noted in his book *Bowling Alone: The Collapse and Revival of American Community* that our "social capital" was diminishing. Between 1975 and 2000, the percentage of Americans joining social and civic groups had dropped 58 percent. Even private socializing had greatly declined: family dinners dropped by 43 percent and having friends over fell by 35 percent.[1] As the title of his book suggested, people were no longer in bowling leagues as a committed group activity but were "bowling alone." This lack of social cohesion, Putnam warned, making us less dependent on one another, could have long-lasting social consequences.

Sadly, his warning largely went unheeded, and social disconnection has become so prevalent that today there is an epidemic of loneliness. In 2019, nearly half of Americans surveyed said they feel isolated and experienced a lack of meaning in their relationships with others.[2] Despite all the social media platforms available to help us stay in touch with one another, we live disconnected and distracted in our relationships with one another. And the impact of this is real.

According to the US Surgeon General, "Loneliness is far more than just a bad feeling—it harms both individual and societal health. It is associated with a greater risk of cardiovascular disease, dementia, stroke, depression, anxiety, and premature death. The mortality impact of being socially disconnected is similar to that caused by smoking up to 15 cigarettes a day and even greater than that associated with obesity and physical inactivity."[3]

Isolation impacts our physical health more than we may be aware of. But it also impacts our relationships and our happiness. How do we increase our social connections? We sense that opportunities for meaningful relationships are diminishing in our communities. More and more events and classes that used to take place in person are being outsourced to online formats. We need to make an effort to see one another for regular social interactions.

The Surgeon General Murthy writes with urgency about our responsibility to combat this epidemic.

> We have . . . an obligation to make the same investments in addressing social connections that we have made in addressing tobacco use, obesity, and the addiction crisis. . . .
>
> If we fail to do so, we will pay an ever-increasing price in the form of our individual and collective health and well-being. And we will continue to splinter and divide until we can no longer stand as a community or a country. Instead of coming together to take on the great challenges before us, we will further retreat to our corners—angry, sick, and alone.[4]

RECLAIMING OUR ABILITY TO RELATE

How we relate to others has undergone a massive change. Screen time for the average American consumer increased at least 50 percent between 2019 and 2021—with some putting the increase as high as 80 percent.[5] One-third of our teens report being on social media "almost constantly," despite 32 percent of teens claiming social media has negatively impacted their lives.[6]

What activities go by the wayside when people are on phones instead of engaging in face-to-face activities? Many things get lost. Conversation becomes less robust and social interactions become more anxiety ridden because of their diminished frequency. Effective communication skills such as interpreting body language, conversing, and emotionally connecting with others continue to decline as people stay behind a screen to "look busy" or to distract themselves. Not surprisingly, depression and anxiety are skyrocketing.

Some explain this rise in mental health issues by claiming that the stigma formerly attached to these things has only recently made it possible for these conditions to be widely reported. However, I think this theory is insufficient to explain the epidemic before us.

Professor D. C. Schindler wrote a pithy and provocatively entitled article, "Social Media Is Hate Speech: A Platonic Reflection on Contemporary Misology." In this article, he explains that the defining characteristic of man is his possession of *logos* (i.e., "reason" or "word"). When a speaker activates his or her capacity for *logos*, it communicates something about reality to the listener. The listener (receiver) must take in the whole of the person, not just his or her words, to judge whether what is said corresponds to reality.

"Language discloses reality," Schindler writes, "and reality is always concrete: the complex, meaning-laden context in which the speaking takes place contributes to the disclosure and so belongs in an intrinsic way to the language."[7]

In other words, communication improves to the degree that the whole person is engaged in conveying the message—a face-to-face conversation is a far more effective way to communicate than, for example, having access to a short clip of an idea conveyed through an audio file or image. Screens are a "medium" that carry their own presuppositions; as we've already discussed, "the medium is the message." It will be increasingly difficult to know whether a person's image via technology is even real, with AI, deepfakes, and the whole new frontier awaiting us.

Writing is a "means of reminding those who know the truth,"[8] and therefore it is not as effective in conveying reality as hearing from and listening to the source directly. Socrates never wrote anything down; he had conversations with people, as that was the way to arrive at truth—through dialogue we come to know. It is better to hear a person in the flesh to judge the truth, rather than just to read their words. This is not to say we should not write or read, but it must be taken into account that the truth is discovered in *relationality*.

Schindler claims that "abstracted from their original source, written words are 'opaque' and so vulnerable to manipulation." And so, when we use social media as the "place for discourse," we are even further removing the person from their speaking. "In [social media's] perfect abstraction from the concrete context of a real speaker, a reality spoken about, and a real listener, these pseudo-intelligible bits are on the one hand cheap, empty, and without bearing constraining purpose and accountability."[9] Therefore, social media is *misology* (*mis*: hatred; *logos*: word) because the platform itself separates the person from the writing by degree and kind.

We all have experienced such phenomena: nasty, anonymous "cyber-trolls" and cyberbullying, contextual misunderstandings from email or text messages. We have seen how even the wearing of masks during the pandemic delayed speech in children because the kids couldn't see their teachers' faces. The human element in communicating truth is fundamental!

In a world where entertainment is king, we have a gazillion streaming platforms and more apps than we know what to do with, all sending a constant stream of dopamine. We are being lured with a false narrative that we need to "keep up" with it all.

But what if we just stopped? What if we intentionally put down our phones with regularity to create a space to engage the world? What if we began to reorient ourselves to live a life with more meaningful connection, and what if happiness involves pursuing wisdom through friendship? What if we left our cell phones at the door and began talking and listening to our families in a more intentional way? What if we made a concerted effort to prioritize relationships that call us to grow?

A VISIT WITH WENDELL BERRY

About ten years ago, I (Colleen) read *Hannah Coulter* by Wendell Berry. I have returned to this work many times over the years. I am fascinated by Berry's portrayal of country life and love that is developed over decades of hard work, quiet nights, and even, at times, boredom. When nothing *appears* new in your life is when you actually have to look at it even harder. It forces you to develop a way of seeing more in the hidden, little things that are right before us.

I decided to write to Wendell Berry and tell him what this novel meant to me. I had heard Mr. Berry lives life differently: He picks up his mail at the post office every day so he can interact with the postal workers. He writes all his novels on paper with a pencil (his wife, Tanya, types them on a typewriter when he's done). He does not buy any newfangled modern luxury items and lives simply, repairing things instead of replacing them. He does not own a computer or a cell phone. He lives connected to the land and its inhabitants.

Imagine my surprise when he wrote back and invited me to his home for a Sunday afternoon visit! I had to write back asking if Marcie and our friend Carla could come along as well, to which he graciously agreed. He gave us directions to his home and warned us, "Now don't follow that GPS thing on your phone, it'll take you clear across town. Look for the mailbox by the hill. Turn at the fork in the road." How fitting that, to find the home of this local pioneer, we actually had to pay attention to the landscape!

We finally made it. Crossing the threshold of his home on the hill, we entered a parlor filled to the brim with books. Then we huddled together in the kitchen around a small table, a bowl full of cherries in the middle, and talked for over three hours. We all concurred that he had cultivated a profound sense of relationality, nurtured over a lifetime, and had a wisdom born not from Twitter but from affection for the real things in his life.

As the conversation continued, Marcie asked, "Mr. Berry, do you ever find it hard to live in such a small town?"

He thought for just a moment and said, "Well, I reckon if I can't find what I'm looking for *here*, I don't suspect I'll be able to find it anywhere, now will I?"

I have returned to that answer many times when I feel the need to be entertained or am tempted to waste time meaninglessly. What is it I'm really looking for? My mother always told me to "bloom where you are planted." In order for something to grow, it must be organically connected with what is around it. We cannot have affection through a screen; we must be present to each other in a new way.

When someone has affection for their home, their place, for others, they come to know themselves more deeply, as Berry observes through the title character in *Hannah Coulter*: "I began to know my story then. Like everybody's, it was going to be the story of living in the absence of the dead. What is the thread that holds it all together? . . . Love is what carries you, for it is always there, even in the dark, or most in the dark, but shining out at times like gold stitches in a piece of embroidery."[10]

FIRST STEPS OF CHANGE

What are some authentic ways to share our lives and build meaningful, personal, face-to-face connections where we live? The steps to strengthen human relationships are simple but real:

📖 Make (or answer) a phone call.

📖 Stop by a friend's house.

📖 Listen intently in conversation (hands-free).

📖 Volunteer in your community.

📖 Share a meal.

And, of course, we would add one more important step:

📖 Read and discuss great and worthy books with others.

> "The best thing to do for one's neighbor is not to give him things to think about, but to wake things up that are in him; or say, to make him think things for himself."
>
> —*George MacDonald*[11]

READING TO COUNTER LONELINESS

In the film *Shadowlands*, when the character of C. S. Lewis comments, "We read to know we are not alone," he is expressing something we long for, an awareness of our connectedness as human beings created in the image of God. This recognition, when it happens, is a gift for us; it counters our loneliness.

We get to know the characters' personalities, strengths, and weaknesses. We witness webs of relationships and social interactions through different time periods. Ideas churn as we ponder sections of the book. We recognize aspects of ourselves in some of the characters. We may ask: "Am I like this? Do I make decisions this way? Will the path this character is taking bring him happiness or lead to his destruction? What path am I on? Is it a path for my happiness or not?"

Through the circumstances of these characters' lives, we experience vicariously what it is like to walk in someone else's shoes. We grow in empathy and gain a deeper understanding of the human condition. We recognize kindred spirits and companions, and like Lewis, we see that we are "not alone."

Stories of a Well-Read Life
A Mother's Grief and *Giants in the Earth*

In 2011 my son Caleb was stillborn at thirty-eight weeks. We were ten days short of his due date when, without warning or cause, his heart stopped beating.

The aftermath of his death was explosive. Grief came raging into my life and I was unprepared for how to handle it. One of the hardest things was the intense feeling of being unseen and unknown in my grief. We have names like "widow" and "orphan," but no name to call a bereaved mother. I felt that namelessness and invisibility down in my soul.

When I read *Giants in the Earth*, I stumbled into a scene that I could instantly relate to. A covered wagon had just rolled up to Per Hansa's home and "inside sat a woman on a pile of clothes, with her back against a large immigrant chest; around her wrists and leading to the handles of the chest a strong rope was tied; her face was drawn and unnatural. . . . To him it looked as if the woman was crucified."[12]

I kept on reading to discover that this woman had watched her son die just days before and had been forced to leave his body behind, buried hastily on the prairie. The only way she would move on from him was if her husband tied her up.

Tears flooded my eyes. This was the same grief I had felt after Caleb died. For months I avoided going to the cemetery after the rain fell for fear that the ground would be too soft and the temptation to literally dig him back up would be too strong. Whenever I went back to the hospital where he was born (and left behind), I had the deep, animalistic urge to tear open all the doors and search endlessly for him. I hadn't shared these feelings with anyone, but here in this book was another woman's life that mirrored the insanity that came with being a bereaved mother.

To this day, *Giants in the Earth* stands as my favorite book because of the comfort I experienced when I encountered this scene. It made me realize that reading doesn't just serve as a hobby or entertainment. It can become a balm to your soul, able to make the deepest, darkest parts of yourself seen and known.—RyAnne Carr

LESSEN LONELINESS THROUGH LITERATURE

What I (Marcie) have found in *my* life—and I hope you will discover, too—is that reading is not (as some might think) an isolating, lonely activity. In fact, it is just the opposite. By engaging in a novel, we choose to slow life down, in order to breathe space into our lives. This space is needed to cultivate meaningful relationships and connections.

Sometimes people read or play video games to avoid relationships. That is not what we are talking about here. When we've taken some time to quiet ourselves down, receive, and contemplate, we have something to say. A solitary activity like reading preps the soil for a fertile conversation (especially if you are reading the same book), which in turn has the potential to foster friendship. And the opposite happens as well: friendships foster reading more. They work together. Friendship holds us accountable to get the reading done, and getting the reading done allows us the opportunity for sharing and connecting in meaningful relationships.

"Everything good in life happens through friendship," a friend once told me.

Again and again, when I look at the beautiful things that have come about for me, I recognize these gifts haven't happened on their own. They have appeared, in part, through friendship and connection.

When our hearts get covered over and we forget who we are and what life is about, friendship can bring us back to our roots. Reading and discussing literature with others also aids in our discovering or remembering who we are. In the process of becoming well read, the ashes covering our hearts are swept away, our hearts lay bare and uncovered and we remember, for a time, who we are. When this happens, we experience a vulnerability, but we also have something to share—if we are only willing to put ourselves out there.

We must be willing to risk, to share at a deeper level. When we do, we realize that we are not alone, friendship grows, and loneliness lessens. My experience over the past thirteen years of reading and discussing literature is one of being helped to experience greater meaning and intensity of life. Rich conversations and regular meetings with friends in a purposeful way is an antidote for loneliness and an experience of deeper belonging and health. I hope that this will be your experience, too.

ACTION STEPS

Answer these questions in your notebook.

- Write about a time you felt lonely. What helped you overcome that feeling?
- Can you recall a time when you read something that made you feel connected, understood?
- Has reading a book ever helped you foster friendship? If so, how?
- What are your most meaningful in-person connections? How can these relationships grow in the upcoming year?
- What do you need to change to make friendship a priority in your life? If you do not feel like this is a strong area in your life, can you identify some people you would like to get to know in a richer way? What steps can you take to strengthen your relationships through greater openness or vulnerability?

CHAPTER 3

An Armchair
REVOLUTION:
Take Back Your Time

"Let your mind become a lens, thanks to the converging rays of attention; let your soul be all intent on whatever it is that is established in your mind as a dominant, wholly absorbing idea."
—A. G. Sertillanges

Approaching literature begins with leisure. Recovering leisure reading as a kind of spiritual discipline will help us move from interior boredom to an expanding inner life. There is not only enjoyment, relaxation, and restoration from this practice but also the shaping and enriching of a Catholic-imaginative view of the world.

What do we need, as human beings? What is it that helps us live our vocations—as spouses, as parents, as workers—in such a way that we thrive? What helps us to be alive in our families, our friendships, and our work? What allows us to continue in our giving and our doing—without burning out amid so many demands? And, if we do experience burnout, how do we get back on track?

One of the things we need is *time to ourselves.*

I (Marcie) used to think of this free time as *my time* to do whatever I wanted: take it easy, take a nap, go out with girlfriends, watch a movie, escape the duties of home life for a little while. But what I've come to understand is this: for free time to be restorative, it needs to include an experience of *leisure.*

If you ask people today why they no longer make time to read (or draw or play music or even pray), a very common answer is "I don't have time." For many people today, reading a novel seems like a luxury they cannot afford in the rat race of modern life. We tend to value "productivity" or "doing/working" over "resting" or "being." For many of us, we see this shift from valuing rest to prioritizing activity particularly evident in how we celebrate (or don't) the Sabbath.

ORDERING YOUR LIFE TO THE RESURRECTION

Sunday used to be a day of rest. Sundays were for going to church, visiting with family, being quiet, and being restored. Most stores were closed on Sunday. Sporting events, particularly for children, did not happen on Sunday as a cultural recognition of having one day of the week—the first day of the week—to give to God in thanksgiving and for contemplating his work in our lives.

In the Gospel of Mark, Jesus reminds us, "The Sabbath was made for man, not man for the Sabbath" (Mk 2:27). In other words, Sunday is a day to remember the Resurrection! This central event in the life of Christians becomes the fact by which all our activities and work find meaning. We pause and reflect on the life Christ has won for us. Our purpose lies not in what we can *produce* but in the meaning and *end* of our work.

WE'VE GOT A PROBLEM

I (Marcie) remember opening St. John Paul II's "Letter to Women" for the first time and reading the following: "Women will increasingly play a part in solving the serious problems of the future: *leisure time*, the quality of life, migration, social services, euthanasia, drugs, health care, the ecology, etc."[1]

While I was completely in agreement that women would have a role in addressing these problems, I was confounded that the first serious problem identified was . . . leisure time.

How is leisure time a *problem*? With the vast array of complex social issues facing our world, the pope was calling women to take part in solving the fundamental problem of leisure time. What did this mean? What was it I needed to understand about leisure?

The nature of leisure must have something to do with forming and shaping our humanity, and the way we share life together. St. John Paul II was concerned that our quality of life is in jeopardy in the modern world. And that quality of life must have something to do with leisure.

A few weeks later, my son Nick came home from college and plopped a stack of books on the kitchen counter. "Mom, here's a book you've got to read," he said, handing me a gem of an essay by Josef Pieper. Startled, I stared at the title, *Leisure: The Basis of Culture*. There was that word again, *leisure*, and Pieper is confidently calling leisure the basis of culture! "This must be what John Paul was referring to," I thought. As I devoured the book, I was introduced to a life-changing, revolutionary understanding of leisure.

AT LEISURE WITH JOSEF PIEPER

Josef Pieper was a twentieth-century German philosopher whose prophetic essay *Leisure: The Basis of Culture* underscored a fundamental problem with our culture: we don't have enough leisure time! Interestingly, this essay was written one year after the word *workaholic* entered our English lexicon.

Pieper argues that leisure is fundamental for religion to flourish, because it prioritizes time spent contemplating the *origin of things*, which necessitates a reference point outside of ourselves and which leads us to God. According to Pieper, time spent reading works of literature is not a luxury to indulge in after all our work is done but an essential starting point for human flourishing.[2]

Do our families experience leisure? What fills our leisure time? Do you feel guilty about sitting down to read a book instead of tackling something on the never-ending "to-do" list? We need to take seriously the lifeline of leisure and restructure our time to give way to contemplation, artistic pursuits, thinking and reading, if we dare to build a culture of hope and love.

Pieper claims that all work has two fundamental aspects, *ratio* and *intellectus*. *Ratio* work is that which is measurable and observable. This is the work that occupies most people's day-to-day lives: plotting, graphing, measuring, shopping, cooking, cleaning, organizing, gathering, and orchestrating. These tasks belong to the *ratio* elements of work and serve to keep our jobs and homes in varying degrees of unity.

The other aspect of work—*intellectus*—requires insight, intuition, and receptivity. These are the moments we intuit, reflect, pray, imagine, read, and create. When we order our time to reflect upon the *intellectus* elements of our lives, we open ourselves to wonder. We can see the higher spiritual plane to which our *ratio* work is ordered and to which it finds its ultimate meaning.

So, what happens when we reduce all work to the *ratio* or measurable work, and don't give time and energy to the metaphysical dimension of our work (*intellectus*)? Cultural decay occurs. We can see signs of this everywhere: from the frantic focus on our children's GPAs instead of the cultivation of curiosity and wonder, to reading for information instead of arousing empathy. Prioritizing the accomplishment of tasks instead of connecting, lingering at the table, and remembering that the people placed in our midst are mysteries to be enjoyed. Our work has a purpose and an end: to rest and to worship. We ought to heed Jesus's instruction to honor the Sabbath.

Genesis reveals to us a foundational truth: everything that exists falls into two categories, the Creator and the created. In his "Letter to Artists," St. John Paul II states, "He who creates bestows being itself, He brings something out of nothing . . . and this, in the strict sense, is a mode of operation which belongs to the Almighty alone. The craftsman, by contrast, uses something that already exists, to which he gives form and meaning. This is the mode of operation peculiar to man as made in the image of God."[3]

Man is made in *imago Dei*—in the image of God; therefore, the study of man, and his history on earth, is really a hunt for God whose image we bear. A writer uses language (a *given* entity) to communicate this truth (knowingly or unknowingly). In this way, a writer can be a craftsman in the sense St. John Paul II spoke of— reading literature becomes a hunt to know the origins of our created self and thus to know God. Language communicates reality, and reality is created by God. Leisure creates a space to contemplate the origins of our very existence, which in turn reveals the meaning of our work. We need to take back our time so as to be "re-created" through leisure to ask the deep questions of our lives.

Any act of work presupposes a gift. For example, the first, most basic principle in cooking is not my activity, my "making," but rather that something there *is* food upon which to act! I (Colleen) did not grow this food or cultivate the seeds. I did not press the oil or ferment the grapes for the wine. Before any action occurs, there is always a *gift*.

I do not plan and prepare a meal to snap an Instagram-worthy picture and produce a "product," but rather to have my family happily gathered around a table. Attuning our hearts to see the work of our hands as an expression of thanks for the gifts God gives us changes the way we approach our work, making it more true and fruitful—and recognizing that something is given implies there must be a Giver.

My family is not the product of *my* effort, *my* work. My family has been *given*, and so I am invited to participate in its cultivation. As Bishop Robert Barron says frequently, "Your life isn't about you." By recognizing this truth, we have a deeper freedom, because our work is a participation in something, not a construction of our own selves. This fundamental recognition allows me to turn my attention to God, the giver of all gifts, and offer him my praise and adoration.

Similarly, leisure is not interchangeable with entertainment or amusement, as I had naively assumed. Leisure, says Pieper, is a "mental and spiritual attitude . . . it is not the *inevitable* result of spare time, a holiday, a weekend, or a vacation."[4] The mere fact that I have free time to do what I want will not restore my soul. I need an openness to hear and perceive the presence of God.

"Leisure," Pieper continues, "is a receptive attitude of mind, a contemplative attitude, and it is not only the occasion but also the capacity for steeping oneself in the whole of creation."[5] Leisure is the way we reconnect to God and the bigger picture of creation, life, and love—the things that really matter. This is the bigger story we are part of, as we are reminded in this Story of a Well-Read Life.

STORIES OF A WELL-READ LIFE
Moments of Fruitful Introspection

I recently had a conversation with my aunt about a book she had read, *Remains of the Day* by Kazuo Ishiguro. In this work, Ishiguro reflects on the life of a butler named Stevens who has spent the better part of his life in service to the lords of the home he serves, Lord Darlington initially, and later Mr. Farraday.

When Mr. Farraday implores Stevens to take a holiday, Stevens takes the master's car on a drive into the English countryside. As soon as he is free from the workaday world of the home, he finds himself stopping at country waysides where memories of his past begin to emerge. Leisure provides him with a much-needed moment to reflect on his own life. He contemplates the choices he has made—prizing duty toward his employer above his own human needs.

My aunt, an octogenarian, reflected on how much she had enjoyed this book because it got her thinking about her own life. Leisure provides introspection. Wayside moments are not idle moments of waste but fertile seeds to nourish and grow.—CH

Pieper calls true leisure an "engaging work." I came to understand that to thrive and have energy to live out my vocation, an "engaging work" of leisure is needed. Suddenly, reading and discussing literature was not just another way to distract myself from my duties; in a sense, it became a duty. Pieper's insight gave me permission to read and contemplate literature—and then to discuss it with my friends. If this is something you crave, welcome to the "armchair revolution"!

AN ARMCHAIR REVOLUTION

As I (Marcie) talk with so many women today, it is hard not to notice the cloud of weariness that hovers over so many of us. In states of near-exhaustion, we keep pressing on. Technology tires us; so do our over-packed schedules. The stress of it all makes us want to weep, but we have no time to weep, let alone sit and read a novel. We have to keep pushing, keep texting, keep posting!

Or do we?

Is there a more beautiful way to live?

Yes! It is possible! If leisure is needed for the growth of our *contemplative inner life*, it is all the more necessary for the living of our *active outer life*.

Therefore, we must *banish guilt* from our experience of leisure. We are not being unproductive when we sit down to reflect and receive. We *are* doing important work! Sit down. Put the phone far away. Allow yourself the freedom to enjoy a story and to be taken to a place the author wishes you to go. The armchair revolution is as simple as making room for surprise and wonder. Start today!

STORIES OF A WELL-READ LIFE
Sharing in Silence

For some of us—especially those extroverts who are energized by other people—sharing our experiences can be an important part of enjoying leisure. A few years ago, when I was in dire need of silence, my friend invited me to attend a silent retreat with her. We had made the retreat together the summer before, and it had been an experience of deep prayer and refreshment. Everything in me wanted to say yes and attend the retreat, and my husband, Pete, was supportive. So why did I hesitate and say no?

The obstacle in my way was the perceived Herculean effort it would take for me to leave the family. I would need to set up childcare, coordinate rides for the kids' tennis and baseball practices, and prepare a few meals in advance. Then there was the uncertainty of Pete's schedule and the six-hour drive to the retreat. Just thinking of finagling the details to bring this forty-eight-hour getaway about had my head reeling. It demanded more energy than I could muster.

"I better stay home," I said to Sarah, a weary note of regret in my voice.

Her response gave me pause: "Well, OK, but remember, creativity follows judgment."

"What do you mean by that?" I asked a bit defensively.

"If you look at your experience from last year's retreat, you made a judgment that the retreat was valuable for your life. You came home happy and renewed in your relationship with the Lord and in family life."

She pulled out her phone and showed me pictures from the retreat. There I sat, smiling and relaxed. Sarah continued, "When you make a judgment that something is worthwhile for your life, you get creative on how to bring it about."

Sarah's honesty jogged my memory. I had told her I wanted to make this silent retreat again if I could. Suddenly a spark of creativity kindled in me. I made a few phone calls, thought through a few simple meals the kids could help make, and before I knew it, Sarah and I were on our way to a much-needed weekend of silence (along with a bag of books, of course!).

Sarah was right. Creativity follows judgment.

What could be more important for our person than to slow down, recognize, and receive the gifts that are easy to miss when our pace of life moves at such a fast speed? When we are intentional about incorporating restorative rituals of leisure into each day, each week, and each month in particular ways, we will reap the benefits of a more ordered, intentional life. Give yourself the gift of restorative leisure.—MS

ACTION STEPS

Answer these questions in your notebook. Becoming well read requires eliminating some nonessentials. By taking a closer look at how we are living, we can make thoughtful decisions about what to keep and what to eliminate.

- How often do you spend leisure time—individually or as a family—at home? Is it set aside as part of our regular routine, or something you enjoy only when everything else is done?
- In this chapter, we talked about the two kinds of work: *ratio* and *intellectus*. Make a list of the kinds of work you do on a weekly basis that fall under each category. Do you dedicate more time to one or the other?
- How do you spend your time? Are there activities you want to include that you are not taking part in now? What can you eliminate to make room?
- In order to make room for leisure time, do you need to set parameters or limits on certain kinds of "screen time"—phone apps, computers, or television? If so, what and when?
- Do you ever feel guilty about making time for leisure? How often do you enjoy restorative leisure—and what form does it take?
- What concrete steps can you take to make restorative leisure a regular part of your day, week, month, and year?

PART TWO

READING TO STRENGTHEN your MIND AND IMAGINATION

"When silence takes possession of you; when far from the racket of the human highway the sacred fire flames up in the stillness; when peace, which is the tranquility of order, puts order in your thoughts, feelings, and investigations, you are in the supreme disposition for learning; you can bring your materials together; you can create; you are definitely at your working point; it is not the moment to dwell on wretched trifles, to half live while time runs by, and to sell heaven for nothings."

—A. G. Sertillanges, *The Intellectual Life*

CHAPTER 4

Engaging a Story with the
Head, Heart,
and Imagination

> "Reason is the natural organ of truth; but
> imagination is the organ of meaning."
> —C. S. Lewis, *Selected Literary Essays*

By reading good and worthy books, we experience vicariously authors' beliefs, experiences, and relationships. As we engage their stories with the mind, with the heart, and ultimately with the imagination, we are able to compare our own circumstances with those in the story with a level of objectivity and detachment. Through this kind of imaginative reading—and subsequent discussion—we are invited to articulate our sense of right and wrong, what is and what ought to be. Deep reading enables us to bridge our own limited experiences with those who have lived throughout varied times and places, deepening our understanding of the world.

*I*n Aristotle's *Metaphysics*, we read, "Animals other than man live by appearances and memories and have but little of connected experience; but the human race lives also by art and reasonings."[1] Living by reason means having certain capacities that help us to understand our experiences. Logical abilities such as deduction, induction, inference, and analysis and synthesis help us process what we receive through our senses.

Engaging our reason helps us to connect our experiences and synthesize them into a connected whole, a narrative. The ability to do this has wide-ranging effects, as Maryanne Wolf points out in *Reader Come Home*: "The careful formation of critical reasoning is the best way to inoculate the next generation against manipulative and superficial information, whether in text or on screen."[2]

In addition to our ability to reason, we have an emotive capacity to feel a wide array of emotions, including pleasure and pain. Both reason and emotion are needed in deep reading: reason makes sense of a novel's structure; emotion allows us to understand what characters experiences. In addition, a third capacity—our imagination—allows us to enter into a story as though it were our own. The imagination is a conduit of meaning from one person to another, the electrical current flowing between what is written on the page as another's experience and our own heart.

CULTIVATE YOUR IMAGINATIVE CAPACITY

> "What we should be seeking are novels that
> can read us, that scandalize us, and cause
> us to trip, fall, and, thus, learn."
> —Jessica Hooten Wilson

Reading a novel is not a race. There are no shortcuts. What matters most is not how many books you get through but experiencing the delight of a book getting through to *you*. When a novel gets through, so does meaning. Imagination is the conduit of meaning. When we cultivate our imagination, we learn, we change, we grow. And as we grow and learn by cultivating our imagination, we begin to change.

The imagination is a capacity of the soul. Like a muscle, it needs to be worked, fed, rested, and exercised on a regular basis. It also needs to be guarded and formed in a moral way. As Orthodox theologian Vigen Guroian has observed, "Much of what passes for moral education fails to nurture the moral imagination. . . . A good moral education addresses both the cognitive and affective dimensions of human nature. Stories are an irreplaceable medium of this kind of moral education. This is the education of character."[3]

So, how can deep, leisurely reading help to build a "moral" imagination?

First, reading good books helps us understand who we are and what motivates us as human beings. National Humanities Medal recipient Myron Magnet argues that a literate public is a force for the common good—and that stories hold the key to understanding who we are and who we may hope one day to become. He writes:

> Literature teaches us more about psychology than the psychologists can. The inner life—and its relation to the outer appearance, from which it is often (and proverbially) very different—is literature's special subject. . . . When a writer imagines his characters' inner drama, his description rings true to us because we have felt similar impulses or imagined analogous situations. . . . We grasp intuitively . . . the simultaneous interplay of feelings, thoughts, beliefs, and

hopes, of conscious and subliminal impulses . . . or sudden insight to impel a character to behave as he behaves.[4]

Second, good books awaken the mind and heart to think and act morally, in accordance with who we were truly created to be. One young scientist, new to reading literature, shared with me (Marcie) this eye-opening insight. "I've taken eighty-four exams to get to where I am in my career," she told me, "but this is a new kind of education. It is an education of my heart." When our imaginative capacity is engaged through story, knowledge is carried to our heart.

Why is this knowledge of the heart so important? So that we grow in awareness of who we are. Carl Jung wrote that one day "the world will ask you who you are. And if you don't know, the world will tell you."[5] We need to know more deeply who we are, our story.

As a Catholic, every time I attend Mass I have the opportunity to enter more deeply into the story I'm part of. I am reminded that I have a Father; I am loved; I belong to Christ. Yet still, it is easy to forget. Our awareness gets covered over by daily concerns, some weighty, most trivial. Without realizing it, we begin to live in a fragmented way, in danger of missing out on an understanding of the whole.

It is through the concrete particulars of a story that universal questions surface, inviting us to contemplate life's bigger questions: Why do I love? Why do I hate? How should I live? What path makes for a beautiful life? Once we begin to see a path forward, we can act.

Stories of a Well-Read Life
Finding God in Russia

When I was in eighth grade, I remember watching a TV evangelist speaking about the Christians behind Russia's Iron Curtain.

"Even if all the Bibles were confiscated," he preached, "the Christian message would remain in the collective consciousness of the Russian people through their literature." The evangelist firmly believed in the power of story to communicate truths of faith and humanity. Woven within the pages of Dostoevsky, Tolstoy, Pushkin, and others, he said, were gospel images of the prodigal son, the Good Samaritan, the Fall, human brokenness, the universal need for forgiveness, and salvation.

I had just finished *God's Smuggler*, a biographical account of Brother Andrew and other missionaries who risked their lives smuggling Bibles behind the Iron Curtain. Now, this TV evangelist confidently preached that even if there were *no* Bibles, the Christian message could be carried to the people through books. I stood awestruck, realizing for the first time that something extraordinarily powerful must be hidden in the pages of these books. If these stories could convert hearts in Russia, I reasoned, reading great books could help me to grow in my faith, too.

Curious about the authors the evangelist mentioned, I investigated one of them, Fyodor Dostoevsky. I found out that Fyodor was a man who knew persecution and oppression firsthand. In 1849, as a young man, he took part in the Petrashevsky Circle, a clandestine literary group that discussed works critical of the czarist regime. Because Dostoevsky and the others read the banned books, they were arrested and soon sentenced to death by firing squad. Clearly, those in power perceived the written word to be a threat to their authority.

In 1849, two days before Christmas Eve, the prisoners were taken to St. Petersburg's Semenovsky Platz to be executed. With rifles pointed at the frightened men, the firing squad stood ready to shoot. But suddenly, something surprising happened. Galloping in, an agent delivered a letter from the czar to the sergeant. The execution was immediately halted. Instead of immediate death, their punishment changed. The prisoners, including Dostoevsky, were sentenced to hard labor.

During their fourteen-day trek to Siberia in Arctic conditions, the weary convicts finally reached a prisoner way station. There, a woman approached Dostoevsky and managed to smuggle him a life-changing treasure—a small New Testament. Fyodor hid the little Bible under his mattress in the barracks of the Siberian labor camp. For four years, he read the gospels over and over. He marked. He underlined. He scribbled in the margins. St. John's gospel was his favorite. He read the New Testament so much the thin pages were nearly worn out. Dostoevsky's deep love of Scripture, coupled with the agonizing experience of injustice and hard labor, forged in his soul a rare and complex grasp of the human condition and the hope and freedom we have as followers of Christ. His novels communicate gospel truths, the human condition, and our universal need for a Savior.—MS

FEEDING AN UNDERNOURISHED IMAGINATION

In our technological age, "seeing" has been diminished as we are led to believe that what is real is what can be quantitatively measured and controlled. Our minds are often wildly oversaturated by snippets of facts and endless feeds of information. We are influenced more than we realize by "facts, nothing but the facts." Our imaginative capacities, including our hearts, are undernourished—and sometimes starving.

As Christians, we know reality is infinitely more than facts. We know that the Lord is present with us, always and everywhere. As we grow in our capacity to see and live in the presence of God, we can find a greater sense of meaning in our ordinary days. One way to nurture our imaginative capacity is to regularly read and discuss great and worthy books, allowing ourselves to dwell on the good and true and beautiful.

What is it about engaging in great and worthy books that holds such promise for our transformation? Holly Ordway writes that literature "provides incremental, gradual, subtle growth; it creates connections that provide for later insights; it establishes meaning that enables further growth."[6] This quiet, hidden kind of learning is profoundly human. When we take part in it, a deeper vision of reality grows. So does our receptivity to the transcendentals—even when they take unexpected forms.

For example, when we tackle a work by Dostoevsky, we gain access to the wisdom and understanding he acquired through his suffering. I (Marcie) experienced this wisdom firsthand when I read the six-hundred-plus-page *Crime and Punishment* for the second time. Because it wasn't my first time through, I knew I'd be entangled for hundreds of pages in the psychological torments of Raskolnikov. Early on, the protagonist commits two brutal murders. For most of the remainder of the novel, I knew I would endure Raskolnikov's heartless, relentless mental torments as he seeks to avoid punishment for his actions.

For days, I continued to ponder the story. Then, I received a surprising flash of insight—*I was like Raskolnikov.* There was a step I needed to take in my life, and I had been avoiding it. I was attempting to step over what I needed to face. It was during the pandemic and had been an intense and challenging year with the sisters in my parish.

My friend and I oversaw the co-op classes that met in our parish. We needed to figure out how to proceed together amid many unknowns. It was a confusing time, and, in the process, we had a falling out, spoke harsh words to each other, and couldn't seem to reach an agreement. A wedge of division entered our relationship. It weighed heavily on my heart and in my mind. I thought about it every day.

Mary and I still waved to each other in passing, and we exchanged small talk on occasion, but the division still lodged in my heart. I went to Confession, asking forgiveness for my anger toward this sister. I prayed and prayed that we be reconciled, but the division remained. Life felt heavy.

After finishing *Crime and Punishment*, I reflected on the unlikeable Raskolnikov's tremendous courage. Finally, he faced what he needed to face and took the step he needed to take. As much as I hated to admit it, he was a hero.

A friend pointed out that one word for crime in Russian is *Prestupleniye*. It means "to step over." A crime is stepping over the law. Throughout most of the novel, Raskolnikov believes he is above God's law. The consequences of his senseless, brutal acts of murder are something he, as an elite, believes he can "step over." Again and again, when Raskolnikov's horrendous crime goes undetected, it seems he will escape the consequences. But his inner torments increase. The reader sees what Raskolnikov, enslaved by his sin, is blind to for so long: you cannot step over God's law and be free.

In a flash, I understood my situation. Like Raskolnikov I was trying to "step over" the action I needed to take—facing my friend. In St. Matthew's gospel Jesus says, "If your brother sins against you, go and tell him his fault, between you and him alone. If he listens to you, you have gained your brother" (Mt 18:15–17).

Suddenly it became clear: "Lord, I've been stepping over what I need to do."

I prayed, "Please give me the courage to go to my sister. I have no idea how to arrange a meeting with her. But if you set it up so Mary and I can meet alone, I will talk with her. But please, will you set it up for us?"

The next morning, I stopped to say a prayer at the Adoration Chapel and guess who was there—*alone*? Tapping her on the shoulder, I whispered, "Mary, may I talk with you for a moment?" She nodded and the words began to flow.

"Mary," I said, "I remember thirty years ago when we moved to this parish, and there had been a conflict over some incident that happened. I never figured out what it was, but I know it created a great deal of division in the parish. I remember thinking, 'They are brothers and sisters in Christ. Why can't they work it out? I would never hold a grudge like that.' Well, during this confusing year, that is just what happened. I think you and I both tried to navigate the best we knew how but, in the process, I said some things I regret. Will you forgive me for the hurtful words I said? I am sorry, Mary. I ask for your forgiveness. Which side of this issue we are on is not what defines us. Our identity is infinitely deeper. We are sisters in Christ; this is who we are."

Mary was in tears. "Marcie, will you forgive me for the way I've hurt you and the words I said?"

There, in the Adoration Chapel, we hugged, and we cried, certain of the power of forgiveness and the joy of reconciliation.

Was spending hours in the pages of *Crime and Punishment* worth my time? Yes, it was! This strange novel, which seemed to have nothing to do with my life, surprisingly opened a window of self-knowledge for me. I was letting the tense situation define my relationship with Mary, telling myself something that wasn't true simply to avoid taking the necessary steps to be reconciled with her.

Like Raskolnikov, who needed to face his crime, I needed to face my sister.

Reading *Crime and Punishment* illuminated what my heart had forgotten: We are made to love and be loved. Asking for forgiveness is necessary for restoration. Through this great work, my imagination was engaged and carried gospel understanding to my heart. I took the step I needed to take, my heart was enlarged, and yes, it *was* worth my time.

AWAKENING THE IMAGINATIVE CAPACITY

Stories shape our view of the world and how it works. Consider what happens when we sit down to read a good book. First, we enter the story. We aren't clicking or making decisions or going anywhere. Instead, we let ourselves travel where the author takes us. As we surrender, there is no need to protect our image or act in a certain way like we may do in other situations. Instead, we relax and surrender to the story. In doing so, without knowing it, we lose ourselves. It is this *losing ourselves* that is essential. It gets us out of the way and allows literature to do its work: cultivating the imagination.

> "The first demand a work of art makes upon us is surrender. Look. Listen. Receive. Get yourself out of the way."
>
> —*C. S. Lewis*

In the process of reading, we're taking in many things: how a character reacts to situations, the choices he or she makes. We are privy to the inner life of the characters and watch them think through situations and make choices. We watch as the consequences that follow those choices unfold. Some decisions are a step toward virtue and goodness; others bring harm to the character and others.

Stories of a Well-Read Life
Good Confessions

At our Well-Read Mom group kickoff meeting for the "Year of the Seeker," we took turns reading a section from St. Augustine's *Confessions*. Finishing the rich narrative, we sat in silence, pondering and receiving the beauty of Augustine's prose.

Then Linda, whose backyard we were sitting in, suggested we walk to the end of her dock and watch the final moments of sunset. Wrapped in blankets and holding mugs of hot tea, eight of us gazed at the shimmering lake, lined with lily pads and cattails. A family of wood ducks paddled silently across the water.

Amy read aloud the first question from the reading companion for us to contemplate: "Both the prose and the poetic sections in the *Confessions* talk about how God's creation points us towards Him. How is creation a signpost towards God as we seek Him in our lives? How do we struggle to read God in the 'book' of creation?"

I'd skimmed over these questions before the meeting and became aware that "reading" God in the book of creation is a struggle for me. I can recognize beauty in nature, but most of the time it seems flat and one-dimensional. I don't often "see" from the psalmist's horizon, where "the heavens are telling the glory of God."

But that night I did. Standing with my friends, watching the lake water reflect black glass, dazzling sparkles, and shimmering lights, for a moment I was graced to see a deeper dimension. Creation, welcoming us; nourishing us with God's love. Could this be what I've heard referred to as a sacramental imagination? That evening, the combination of the reflective silence, St. Augustine's prose, and the beauty of nature primed and opened my heart to a greater, more complete experience of reality. I could see the bigger story I am part of and recognized with St. Augustine, "Our hearts are restless until they rest in You." Goodness, truth, and beauty were unified, and my imagination awakened to a deeper, truer, infinite dimension of reality, a sacramental way of "seeing."—MS

ACTION STEPS

📖 Next time you read a work of fiction, create a mental space to think about the setting, the characters, and the characters' action. Let your mind wander. Imagine what their day-to-day life is like. Why does a character make certain decisions? What led them there? Enter their story by using your imagination to "fill in the gaps."

📖 Engage your senses. Feel the landscape. Taste the food they eat. Hear the sounds each character listens to. How does building empathy for a character change your experience of the novel or poem?

📖 Think of a time when you had to push yourself to finish reading something. Was there a particular character or scene that tripped you up or caused you to lose interest? Does Marcie's account of *Crime and Punishment* remind you of an analogous situation in your own life?

CHAPTER 5

Choosing
Books
That Change Us

> "Mere instruction in morality is not sufficient
> to nurture the virtues. It might even backfire.
> . . . Instead a compelling vision of the goodness
> of goodness itself needs to be presented in a way
> that is attractive and stirs the imagination."
> —Vigen Guroian[1]

When it comes to evaluating the quality of literature, we must test it out, make a judgment. Will reading this book help you grow in your humanity and your capacity to see and understand yourself and others? If so, make space for this gift and give yourself permission to read.

Avoid being too harsh in your judgments. When a friend was feeling guilty about reading novels rather than "spiritual books" with us, her spiritual director gave this counsel: "If something you take part in is making you more of who God made you to be, give yourself permission to stay with it." In this chapter, we will learn how to take this good advice to heart.

$\mathcal{G}$ood books have the power to transform us—once we become willing to commit to establishing a regular reading practice. At this point, the details of that commitment don't need to be set in stone; success looks different for every person. If you have a full-time job in addition to any home or family responsibilities, success might be starting with one or two books a year and building from there. Cathedrals were not built in a day! We need to attune our minds, our hearts, and our time to accommodate this new endeavor. Be patient with yourself but choose your content wisely.

What does it mean to read "great and worthy" books? Knowing *which* books to read is the first step. With an almost inexhaustible amount of literature being published, it can be difficult to know where to start.

Dorothy Day—a voracious reader—made this recommendation: "Turn off your radio. Put away your daily paper. Read one review of events a week *and spend some time reading [good books]*."[2] She recognized a connection between reading literature and growing in a life of faith.

Louise Cowan explains the importance of great books in terms of "reinstructing" the mind. "Classics don't tell us what we already know. They remind us of something the heart knows. We don't live by our hearts most of the time. We live by our minds, and the mind needs to be continually reinstructed because it tends to go off by itself and make its own systems. So, classics surprise us by making us see truth in a new light. And at the same time, it's something radically new and yet something old and hidden and forgotten."[3]

So what makes a work of literature "great"? What is the difference between a classic and a book that is simply . . . old?

WHAT ARE "GREAT BOOKS"?

The official canon of the "great books" has evolved over the last century, comprising a list of the foundational texts of Western civilization, which conventionally date from the late eighth or early seventh century BC through the mid-twentieth century. These works span a wide range of inquiry from philosophy, theology, political science, psychology, history, and the sciences to music and language—including epic poems and plays, precursors of the modern novel. (Most people consider *Don Quixote*, written by Miguel Cervantes in 1605, to be the first modern novel.)

What makes a book great? Some common criteria are that it has stood the test of time, has had an impact on culture, has artistic merit, and that it reveals something fundamental about the human condition or nature. For our purposes, we are going to concentrate primarily on works of literature.

In the early 1920s the American university system began to focus on area-specific training and research instead of a common intellectual grounding. This was largely in response to a clamor for "useful" education to prepare students for the "real world" (rather than "theoretical learning" that had little to do with productivity). In her essay "Poetry, Imagination and Education," Amy Lowell writes, "More and more . . . has the old education by means of the humanities been broken down. . . . Children are taught to do, where, in the older systems, they were taught to think."[4] In terms of investment value, money spent on education (or time spent on leisure) was considered worthwhile to the degree that it was intrinsically related to "production" or "utility." However, when time and work are separated from the contemplation of the most essential things in life (God, creativity, growing in goodness, cultivating the truth, and appreciating the transformative power of beauty), our understanding of life becomes malnourished.

The modern great books canon as we know it began in 1919 at Columbia University when Professor John Erskine offered his first General Honors class to combat the trend of trade-specific courses that were disconnected from a "liberal" or general education. Erskine had two prominent students, Robert Hutchins and Mortimer Adler, who would continue to champion the idea of a holistic education based on the medieval *trivium* and *quadrivium*. Hutchins became the president of the University of Chicago, and Adler would join him there as a professor of law and later as chairman of the *Encyclopedia Britannica*. Others would pick up the great books banner: Allan Bloom, Otto Bird, and later William Bennett. These men had varied political and religious backgrounds, but they all saw the importance of reading to educate the mind and the heart.

The great books canon has gone through several iterations over the last hundred years. The University of Chicago's Basic Program of Liberal Education, the University of Notre Dame's Program of Liberal Studies, St. John's College (an institution exclusively focused on the great books), and many others have much overlap in what they require students to read across various disciplines.[5]

In more recent years, there has been a recognition of the need to include more ethnic diversity in the canon. While the books that have shaped Western history up to this point do show diverse perspectives (reading Plato from fifth-century BC Greece is vastly different from reading Victor Hugo in eighteenth-century France), the vast majority of entries in the original canon were written by European males. So efforts have been made to expand the list to include works by men and women of non-European descent, recognizing the importance of sharing the world stage with those unique voices and perspectives. By including these voices without dismissing or negating the traditional canon of ancient literature, the golden thread of ideas and insights is carried forward, not just cut off from the past out of which it has grown.

Of course, many contemporary works of literature possess artistic merit and reflect a deep understanding of the human person and are rightly classified as "worthy" books—especially those written by authors of color and women writers who have been underrepresented in the traditional canon of great books. When *To Kill a Mockingbird* by Harper Lee or *Their Eyes Were Watching God* by Zora Neale Hurston first emerged on the literary scene, their works were misunderstood, criticized, and even banned. But now we can see these works of literature as tremendous gifts. They have added missing voices regarding the human experience.

CHOOSING BOOKS THAT SHAPE THE MORAL IMAGINATION

When selecting books, should we avoid those that contain overt acts of sensuality or violence? How does what we read inform and influence both our conscience and our sense of morality? Like a garden cultivated with rich, organic compost, when we read books of an elevated artistic merit, we will grow in our humanity. Having fed our minds with nutrient-dense material, we will not settle for "smut and twaddle" books that glare forth with neon lights, trying to hook readers by voyeurism, explicit content, or cheap ideology.

This does not mean, however, that we should wall ourselves within a garden where only the most beautiful, virtuous literary fruits grow. Transformation happens through suffering. The key difference is whether the author wallows in depravity *as* depravity or celebrates sin for its own sake, or instead allows us to see depravity and sin for what they really are. The cross Jesus hung upon is a violent reminder of the depth of love, not just a macabre image. This is the literary principle we apply to reading works depicting difficult subject matter.

Neither will we be satisfied with simplistic, reductionist "morality plays," with two-dimensional characters and unimaginative or forced plotlines. In the classic seventeenth-century allegory *Pilgrim's Progress*, the characters made choices that were clear-cut and had predictable outcomes. However, this is usually not the way we come to know things on the deepest level or are guided to reflect upon our own behavior or moral standards.

Artistic literature *shows* us (rather than tells us) how to live. In the words of Well-Read Mom companion editor Carla Galdo, "We seek to read not works that glorify a sinful life, but rather those that illuminate our deepest need: our need for a Savior to enter into our life and claim it. Just as Christ didn't turn away from the wounded Samaritan woman at the well, knowing well the scandalous behavior that shadowed her past and her present, we cannot circle our wagons of virtue and close ourselves off from the world's flaws—primarily because the most pernicious brokenness dwells not outside our front door, but within our hearts."[6]

So, what are some of the most important characteristics to consider in choosing the books we read?

LIKE A THORN IN THE HEART

In a May 2023 address to poets and writers in Rome, Pope Francis claimed, "Literature is like a thorn in the heart; it moves us to contemplation and sets us on a journey."[7] His words reminded me (Colleen) of a book I'd recently read that felt like a "thorn in my heart." In *Giants in the Earth* by O. E. Rölvaag, the reader experiences the challenges that the immigrant pioneers faced as they headed west to build their new life on the American plains. We journey alongside Per Hansa and Beret as they sacrifice and toil to build a home through plagues, drought, hardship, and death. Reading this book made the sacrifice of generations past come alive and made me contemplate things I tend to take for granted.

It is this quest for meaning and purpose that characterizes the moral imagination. It is something that cannot be derived from watching the movie or reading the CliffsNotes, can't be broken down into parts and fragments of information. These books elevate our minds and cause us to see the whole, shedding light and transparency on the meaning of things.

Reading *Giants in the Earth*, I could not help but compare my life to that of Per Hansa and Beret and recognize that I live a life of bounty: I never had to clear the earth or dig up stones to build my home by hand. I have food to eat that is not dependent solely and directly on my planting and harvesting. Everything that has been given to me every day, my ancestors had to earn by the sweat of their brow. Even my faith was handed down to me from generations past. As I contemplated the journey of the pioneers in that novel, a sense of gratitude came alive in my heart.

Books can take us on all kinds of emotional and psychological journeys. A few years ago, a woman I will call "Emily" shared with me her story of reading *A Raisin in the Sun*. Emily had been having a challenging time with her teenage daughter, "Lauren." Lauren had started to use drugs, steal from her parents, and engage in risky sexual behavior. When they tried to restrict her access to these things and seek the help of a counselor, Lauren would often run away. For days at a time, Emily would have no idea where Lauren was or if she was safe. It was a terrifying position to be in.

Things deteriorated over the course of a few years, until the parents had to seek help from the courts to try and get Lauren to comply with commonplace rules of the home. One afternoon, Emily was reading *A Raisin in the Sun* when she got a call from her daughter's assigned social worker. She had reason to believe Lauren was using drugs again, and the social worker asked Emily to search Lauren's room. She put her book down, went into Lauren's room, and searched it with a fine-tooth comb. Emily found drugs, alcohol stolen from their locked cabinet, and several items taken from her own bedroom. She began to cry. She shared the thoughts racing in her head with me. "Why was this child so difficult? Why did she continue to put herself in dangerous situations? Why couldn't she just obey us, her parents who loved her so much? Why can I not get through to her? Why? Why? Why?"

Emily was overwhelmed and exhausted trying to help Lauren and build a relationship with her. After cleaning up all the paraphernalia and documenting everything for the court, Emily returned to her book. When she picked it up, she was surprised by the words on the page at the exact spot where she had left off:

> Mama: I thought I taught you to love him.
> Beneatha: Love him? There is nothing left to love.
> Mama: There is *always* something left to love. And if you ain't learned that, you ain't learned nothing. . . . Child, when do you think is the time to love someone the most? When they done good and made things easy for everybody? Well then, you ain't through learning— because that ain't the time at all. It's when he's at his lowest and can't believe in hisself 'cause the world done whipped him so![8]

In this scene, Walter Jr. loses some of the money he inherited from his father in a get-rich-quick scheme. This hard-won money was supposed to have been used to buy a new house in a better neighborhood for the struggling Black family. Now those hopes were dashed. And it was at this specific moment, Mama could see, Walter needed to be loved back into the family.

In an instant, Emily saw her daughter in a new light as the words leapt from the page and directly into her heart. She needed to keep loving—even when her daughter was at her worst, even if the relationship didn't transform overnight. Somehow, Mama's experience made it easier for Emily to pick up her own cross and keep going. This image, this scene, showed Emily the courage and trust required to love through disappointment.

In this spirit, here are some guideposts along our journey to come to know ourselves and judge our actions in view of the complex mystery of the human person.

READ TO BROADEN YOUR UNDERSTANDING OF LIFE

Before you begin to read great books, your understanding is limited to your own time and place. Your worldview is rather skeletal and limited. But as you choose books about unfamiliar times and places, you begin to clothe the skeleton. Ideas develop as history is enfleshed through art, story, and language.

Books have changed the trajectory of peoples and nations, their language, art, and history. It is hard to overstate the importance that Dante's *Divine Comedy* had on the development of the Italian language, on poetry, and on theology. Or how Homer's *Odyssey* influenced poetry, the development of Greek (and subsequently Western) culture and religion, literature, and the model of the hero's journey.

G. K. Chesterton reminds us of the importance of reading your "ancestors"—those who have gone before us and have much to say to us today. When you read books from different time periods you can enter the worldview they had at the time.

> Tradition means giving a vote to the most obscure of all our classes, our ancestors. It is the democracy of the dead. . . . Tradition refuses to submit to the small and arrogant oligarchy of those who merely happen to be walking about. All democrats object to having men being disqualified by the accident of birth; tradition objects to their being

disqualified by the accident of death. Democracy tells us not to neglect a good man's opinion, even if he is our groom; tradition asks us not to neglect a good man's opinion, even if he is our father.[9]

When I read *Shadows on the Rock* by Willa Cather, I was stunned by the incredible witness of the Canadian martyrs of the seventeenth century. Cather describes one such person, Noël Chabanel. Cather writes that "his martyrdom was his life, not his death." Fr. Chabanel was a professor of rhetoric in France and was fond of refined things, artfully crafted culinary delights, intelligent discussion, poetry, art, and so on. He gave up the fineries of life to become a missionary to the Huron Indians in Canada.

Enduring nearly constant torture, mockery, and privation, Chabanel wrestled with the temptation to go back to France and return to his life of books, French cookery, and friends. And yet, on the Feast of Corpus Christi, he chose to make a vow of perpetual stability to the Huron missions. Two years later, he was martyred. Cather reminds us, "But Noël Chabanel—ah, when your faith is cold, think of him! How can there be men in France today who doubt the existence of God, when for the love of Him, weak human beings have been able to endure so much?"[10]

Reading the horrific account of his daily brutalities made me look at the liturgical calendar of the Church in a new way. I finally realized *this* man, whose feast day is October 19 (along with Sts. John de Brébeuf, Isaac Jogues, and Companions) gave up everything he loved not just at the moment of his death but for many excruciating years leading up to that moment. He died to bring the faith to this continent.

This novel awakened in me a desire to give up more for the Lord. To say yes to the things God asks of me and to be so grateful for the entire tradition of witnesses who have gone before me so I could be given the faith. Since reading that novel seven years ago, I get *Shadows of the Rock* down from the shelf every October 19 and reread the section pertaining to Chabanel's story. I examine what I am truly giving to Christ. This moment of pause has been an incredible source of fruitfulness in my spiritual life. This story was a gift of understanding tradition in a new way for me.

Our faith, our thinking, our way of life come to us from a point of origin outside of ourselves. Reading great books helps us to understand this on the level of the heart.

READ BOOKS TO EXPERIENCE MEANING

There is just something about a story. When Jesus wanted to teach us something of immense value, like mercy, he leaned on parables to convey the message. Listening to the parable of the prodigal son, we were not just *told* to be merciful but *given an image* of what mercy looks like.

A story is more than a simple lesson; it involves the *mystery* of the human person. Flannery O'Connor says, "The writer operates at a peculiar crossroads where time, place, and eternity somehow meet. His problem is to find that location. . . . A story is a way to say something that can't be said any other way, and it takes every word in the story to say what the meaning is. You tell a story because a statement would be inadequate. When anybody asks what a story is about, the only proper thing is to tell them to read the story.

The meaning of fiction is not abstract meaning but experienced meaning."[11]

Meaning becomes incarnate in words—in language—through a complex tapestry of thought, plot, action, climax, resolution, character, theme, setting, foreshadowing, symbol, and analogy. These tools of writing, in the hand of a master, can be crafted to convey the depths of human experience.

A few years ago, I had a profound experience of mercy inspired by the book *Return of the Prodigal Son* by Henri Nouwen. I was coleading a pilgrimage to the Shrine of Our Lady of Champion in Wisconsin (one of only eleven Vatican-approved Marian shrines in the world!) with Marcie, and after thirty-eight miles and two days of walking and sleeping on the floors of parish basements, we arrived at the shrine for Mass. During the homily, Bishop David Ricken of the Diocese of Green Bay spoke about the pain we suffer when our family is incomplete, specifically when our children are not practicing the faith. Bishop Ricken urged us to *name* the people closest to us who have left the Church and to ask the Lord for their return, a beautiful practice I have kept alive at every Communion I have received since that day.

In his book *The Return of the Prodigal Son*, Nouwen travels to St. Petersburg to visit the Hermitage Museum, which houses Rembrandt's famous painting of the same name. Nouwen spent hours, day after day, meditating on this particular work, gleaning from the painting spiritual truths that slowly began to take root in his soul. Nouwen eventually realized he had played the part of all the characters in this familiar parable. At times, he had been the insolent son, leaving the father behind to take his place in the world and satisfy his worldly desires. At other times, he had been the judging older son who kept the balance of the other's sins in the iron ledger of his heart, not delighting in conversion but placing himself above reproach with arrogance and pride. But, as Nouwen comes to discover, we are really called to be the father, to outstretch our hands to all who return home.

As I walk up to the Lord to receive Communion, I think of *The Return of the Prodigal Son*. I am returning to the Father through Christ. I am begging him to help draw those I know and love who have left the Church back to the Father's loving embrace through my prayer of supplication. This book brought to life the bishop's words by giving me an image to follow as I walk up to receive the Body of Christ. This book has been a source of mercy for me because I, too, have played all the roles of the prodigal son. As I have received mercy, I am called to be merciful. The Father longs for me to keep praying for the conversion of all who are far from Him and to be spiritually ready to receive them with the greatest of joy when they make the journey home.

The intensity of the image we are given correlates to the artistic capability of the writer. When I look back over the books that have impacted me the most, I remember specific scenes or moments, seared in my heart, to help me react to the demands of life. Of all the images that have been meaningful to me, I do not believe there will ever be one as sacred for me as the father embracing the lost child.

READ TO UNDERSTAND THE HUMAN CONDITION

In his beautiful "Letter to Artists," St. John Paul II said, "Even in situations where culture and the Church are far apart, art remains a kind of bridge to the religious experience."[12] Art has a way of inhabiting the deepest parts of a person, regions both resplendent and shadowed.

I witnessed art as a bridge to a religious experience while reading *The Picture of Dorian Gray* by Oscar Wilde. This is not a religious work, and Wilde himself had a complicated relationship with faith. He admitted, "To go over to Rome would be to sacrifice and give up my two great Gods: Money and Ambition."[13] And yet, all his life he would feel the ache for God.

Wilde wanted to convert to Catholicism in his adolescence, but his father refused. He attended university and got married. He had several children but wrestled with seeking pleasure and began to pursue homosexual relationships. Eventually, Wilde was convicted of sodomy and sentenced to two years of hard labor.

While in prison, Wilde read Dante, Augustine, and Newman, and upon release he applied for a six-month retreat with the Jesuits but was denied. Instead, he wandered Europe, mostly penniless. He even went to Rome and had an audience with Pope Pius IX, who told Wilde, "I hope that you may take a journey in life in order to arrive at the city of God." Toward the end of Wilde's debauched life, his longtime friend Robbie Ross called for a priest, and the dying Wilde was received into the Catholic faith on his deathbed.

So how is this grappling for truth reflected in Wilde's *Picture of Dorian Gray*? And what is it about that journey that makes it "worthy"?

Dorian Gray is an attractive, wealthy, indulgent young man who, at the zenith of his virility and beauty, is presented with a portrait of himself. Seeing how beautiful his image is and knowing that someday he will lose his youth and beauty, he vows he would "give his soul" if the picture could age and he remain young.

As the novel progresses, we see Dorian gets his wish but not in the way he intended. Outwardly, Dorian stays remarkably young and beautiful as he plunges himself into a hedonistic life one sin at a time. The portrait, however, bears the disfigurement of his soul. Over time, it becomes a grotesque image barely recognizable as the visage of a once-beautiful man.

At our discussion, the women saw in *The Picture of Dorian Gray* a true representation of the unrepentant soul. Sin disfigures and Confession heals—erases—the marks of our disfigurement. As we considered the sins of our own lives in light of Wilde's portrait, it spoke to our hearts in a tangible way. Afterward, several women confided in me that, because of reading that book, they went back to the Sacrament of Confession after having been away from it for years. They could see in Wilde's image of Dorian's disfigured portrait what sin does to the soul.

Through literature, even those people who don't consider themselves "religious" can find themselves opened to the religious sensibilities that permeate their lives. The books we read allow us to ask the important questions of life through the lives of the characters. What does it mean to be human? What are the "goods" I should be seeking in life? How do we live in a fallen world? What gives life meaning?

READ TO UNCOVER LIFE'S PARADOXES

Literature can often reflect the paradoxical tensions of the world back to us. We live in a world that is both a "vale of tears" and a wellspring of God's grace. We strive, seek, love, and suffer in this world, yet we long for heaven. We must live "in" the world but not be "of" it as we journey through this life, east of Eden, and we know God's goodness will triumph even amid the sin around us.

At the same time, it is important to realize that while some books have scenes of depravity or characters that are despicably fallen, it is important not to seek out books that glamorize evil or fail to see evil *as* evil. This is a key distinction! One can read with confidence books that reveal the ugliness and brutality of this life, if these are placed within a larger framework of reference. Servant of God Luigi Giussani says, "The educational method with the greatest capacity for good is not the one that flees reality in order to affirm what is good separately, but rather the one that lives by advocating for the triumph of good in the world."[14]

This insight came alive for me as we read John Steinbeck's novel *East of Eden*. *East of Eden* deals with the reality of evil head-on. This semi-autobiographical novel is about the Trask and the Hamilton families (Steinbeck's mother was Olive Hamilton), as they journeyed west to start new lives in the promised land of California's Salinas Valley. Several of the characters are despicable, including Cyrus and Charles Trask, but one is just about pure evil: Cathy/Kate Trask.

As the good people and the bad grew up alongside each other, characters like Adam thought it was within their reach to make of this world their own Eden. Those illusions come crashing down upon the characters, who wrestle with the brilliance and darkness in the heart of each person. Steinbeck's title refers to the actual place Adam and Eve were banished after their fall: "Therefore the

LORD God sent him forth from the garden of Eden, to till the ground from which he was taken. He drove out the man; and at the east of the garden of Eden he placed the cherubim, and a sword flaming and turning to guard the way to the tree of life" (Gn 3:23–24, NRSV).

In this book, Steinbeck wrestles with the spiritual geography we find ourselves in, living east of Eden. While created *very good*, after the fall of man our intellects were darkened and our wills weakened. Goodness and evil both dwell in our hearts now. The Church teaches that the extraordinary grace of Baptism remits all sin—and this is incredible news! The *Catechism of the Catholic Church* (*CCC*) states that "nothing remains that would impede [the newly baptized person's] entry into the Kingdom of God, neither Adam's sin, nor personal sin, nor the consequences of sin, the gravest of which is separation from God" (1263).

After Baptism the consequences of sin remain, "such as suffering, illness, death, and such frailties inherent in life as weakness of character, and so on, as well as the inclination to sin that the Tradition calls concupiscence" (*CCC*, 1264). Yet we must remember this was *not* the beginning of the story—we were made *very good*, to live naked without shame and dwell in the garden and have dominion over it (without toil!).

Of course, after the banishment, the human story devolved quickly, producing lies and murder in one generation. The history of Cain and Abel is visible around us daily. When Steinbeck was crafting Cathy's character, he commented, "You open up the morning paper and you will find a dozen stories of people who have done things which are not true to you because they are not in our experience. Yesterday a grown boy killed both of his parents because they would not let him use the car."[15]

Why did this boy kill his parents? Why does Cathy make some of the choices she makes? Steinbeck is asking us to think about the nature of sin. It will not make us more virtuous people if we ignore the evil in the world. We must face it. We must recognize it *as* evil. Standing before evil rightly makes us uncomfortable. This is what Steinbeck helps us to see.

We live *in this fallen world*. We cannot build our own paradise, because we are broken on the most fundamental level. We are not God. We cannot redeem flesh from death. We cannot return to a prelapsarian state of no pain, no suffering, and no sickness. But God did give us one extraordinary power—freedom! After the Fall, much was lost, but we are reminded that in Christ and through grace our freedom can be made perfect by directing it toward God more perfectly. We are not condemned!

We can choose our actions, our attitudes, our affections. When freedom becomes most alive in us, our choosing becomes oriented totally toward the good. The drama of human life consists in the playing out of these choices. The Hebrew word *timshel*—"Thou mayest"—Steinbeck suggests, "might be the most important word in the whole world. That says the way is open,"[16] but it is up to us to decide. Sometimes it is an unbearable weight to accept the choices of another person, especially when they bring about their own destruction.

It can be a challenge to read a book with "bad" things in it. Sometimes we want the Hallmark version of reality. Flannery O'Connor once said, "What people don't realize is how much religion costs.

They think faith is a big electric blanket, when of course it is the cross. It is much harder to believe than not to believe."[17]

If you draw this position out to its extreme, there would hardly be anything left to read, including the Bible! Abraham, our father in faith, did not trust God when he found himself in Egypt and allowed his wife Sarai to be taken as concubine of the Pharaoh. Awful. Lot's daughters committed incest with Lot to further their progeny after they were saved from Gomorrah by a message from an angel. How is that for a thank-you to God for rescuing them!

Fortunately, that was not the whole story. Dante's *Inferno* is full of people who have done awful, horrific things. Even the beloved *Kristin Lavransdatter* by Sigrid Undset would not meet some standards of morality, because Kristin had premarital sex, which is clearly forbidden by God's law. We don't dwell in the Inferno, but it is a real place—in fact, one we must journey through to get to heaven. If we put *Kristin* aside after a few chapters, we would miss how a fallen, sinful person like Kristin (like me!) could be transformed over a lifetime into who God really made her to be.

The Bible is our history, and it details the immense sins of the world: from worshipping idols to taking the Lord's name in vain, adultery, rape, prostitution—you name it and that sin is in the Bible. But the point is not to entice us to evil but to show us the error of a freedom divorced from truth. The point of recognizing evil in a work of great literature is to guard against it, to battle it, to counsel others toward something else (think of Samuel and Lee in *East of Eden*—extraordinary characters!).

The *Catechism* is profound on this point: "Sin is present in our human history; any attempt to ignore it or to give this dark reality other names would be futile. To try and understand what sin is, one must first recognize the *profound relationship of man to God*, for only in this relationship is the evil of sin unmasked in its true identity as humanity's rejection of God and opposition to him, even as it continues to weigh heavy on human life and history" (386). Steinbeck's *East of Eden* is exploring, in a literary way, the profound relationship of man to God. Cathy/Kate meets the outcome of her errant ways and warped freedom in the destruction of *her very self*. Much like Dorian Gray. Much is at stake in the small amount of time each of us is given on this earth.

Every person has a history to be considered, however. If certain topics or scenes would be too much for a particular reader, one should follow their conscience and refrain from reading them. But abstaining from some selected reading because of a person's personal history and sensitivities is different than trying to avoid the ugly realities of life. The goal is to read in a way that is not voyeuristic but transformative.

Stories of a Well-Read Life
Hard Yet Fruitful Lessons

When we read literature, we consider hard questions. What should the character have done? What would I do in his situation? Which character do I want to emulate? For what must I repent?

I found myself forced to face these questions recently as I read *East of Eden*. I loved so much about this masterpiece of literature, which, though full of depravity and ugliness, called me to greater virtue. I could not read the book at arm's length; instead, I clutched it tightly, captivated. Steinbeck's masterpiece absorbed me from the first chapter's gorgeous descriptions of the Salinas Valley. Like the very best of books, it sent me, over and over again, to prayer, my Bible, and the sacraments. And in the most uncomfortable yet incredibly healing way, it held up a mirror to help me see myself in a new way.

While (like many readers) I immediately hated Cathy/Kate and loved Samuel Hamilton, I most identified with Adam Trask, because of his experience with hardship (though his circumstances were much different from mine). Nearly one year ago, my family was in a severe car accident, hit head-on one afternoon while driving my four boys from the library to a friend's house.

Praise be to God, we all survived this terrible incident. And yet the wounds of this car crash went deep. Like Adam, after Cathy shot him and ran off, I spent much of the past year feeling sorry for myself. So, when Samuel Hamilton confronts Adam—first punching him when Adam refuses to name his boys and then reprimanding Adam for leaving his land fallow—I was struck to the core.

I had indeed "take[n] pride in [my] hurt." Like Adam, I was "playing a part on a great stage with only [my]self as an audience."[18] Reading these words made me see myself and my situation clearly and helped me recognize my lack of freedom due to my pain. I didn't want to see this. I didn't want to be Adam. I wanted to be Lee, Adam's Chinese American servant.

No stranger to tragedy himself, Lee faithfully serves Adam. In raising the boys, keeping the house, and cooking for the family, Lee plays the role of the missing wife and mother. Lee looks outside of himself and makes time to cultivate his own intellectual life. Doing so, he says, makes him a man.

I so admired this, and wanted to serve my own family with love, listening deeply to those around me and bringing out the best in others, all while letting go of my selfishness—just like

Lee does. His example was a powerful reminder that we have a choice. We can choose freedom and forgiveness.

In the months following our accident, our family prayed for forgiveness and healing for the man who hit us, but in a way that felt very abstract. Then, when I went last month to his sentencing hearing (to advocate for probation instead of incarceration), I got to see the man who hit us for the first time since he was carried away from the accident unconscious on a stretcher. He was no longer a theoretical "enemy" that I was commanded to love and pray for in the abstract. He was a real flesh-and-blood image-bearer.

Upon seeing him, my heart filled with compassion and love. I delivered my victim impact statement and then was able to look him in the eyes and assure him of our family's forgiveness. Through that forgiveness, I experienced freedom. It was one of the most beautiful moments of my life, all a result of something so ugly, which occurred because of the fallenness of our world.

Our world is fallen; we live east of Eden. And yet, as Christians, we know that there is redemption in our suffering. There is hope in tragedy. The darkness cannot overcome the light. This knowledge enables us to bear real-life sufferings and enter even the darkest stories. We need not shy away from reality, including from good books that portray its fallenness.

Sometimes we need a punch in the face. I, for one, would much rather it come from a book than from real life. This wisdom is one of the many compelling reasons to read hard books. They can help us practice for things we have yet to experience in real life (many of which we pray we never do), awaken us to reality, and invite us to freedom. This power of great literature—especially literature read in community with one another—is offered to us if we are courageous enough to see and receive it.—Nicki Johnston

ACTION STEPS

📖 Find yourself a good and worthy book! As you peruse the bookshelves, ask yourself:

- Why do I want to read this work? Has someone recommended this book to me? Does it have artistic merit? Is it well written?
- Will this book stretch me intellectually? Will it help grow and nurture my humanity?
- Does this book depict sin and violence graphically or gratuitously? Is this book voyeuristic?
- Don't forget to acquire a journal or notebook and highlighters to keep track of what you learn as you read!

📖 What are books that made a vivid impression on your "moral imagination" when you were growing up? Why not reread one of them, and rediscover why they made such an impression?

📖 Can you identify a few powerful images or characters from literature that have impacted how you respond to situations in your life? What moved you? How has this image or character shaped you?

📖 What are some areas in which you think you need to cultivate a stronger sensibility or awareness and build up your moral imagination? Name some virtues or habits you would like to develop.

📖 Examine *why* you read. Is it to "escape" from reality or "enter into" reality more deeply? What kind of books do you gravitate toward? Did anything you read in this chapter challenge you to broaden your selection criteria?

CHAPTER 6

I Have a
Book
. . . Now What?!

> "I was taught that the way of progress
> was neither swift nor easy."
> —Marie Curie

This chapter offers practical tips and strategies to sharpen your skills for focused reading and greater comprehension. Books can be our friends and also our teachers. Don't be afraid to ask questions, read summaries, annotate your texts, and journal intentionally in order to collect and retain wisdom.

The second part of this chapter includes strategies to keep your motivation high and your awareness alert, and to avoid potential pitfalls that can sabotage your success. By being intentional and aware, you will grow in your reading skills, comprehension, and enjoyment of literature.

*F*or me (Marcie), becoming well read means becoming a regular reader. The good news is that, as we develop a reading practice, we become well read in the process!

Rebuilding our reading habits can be a bit like rebuilding muscle through weight training. And, as with weight training, it helps to have a "trainer." Hopefully, this book will serve in this capacity for you, and you'll be on your way to regular reading once again or for the first time. (If you want to take things even further, why not join Well-Read Moms?)

So . . . how to start? It all starts with making a commitment—and keeping it.

GOOD INTENTIONS ARE NOT ENOUGH

"The person who doesn't read has no advantage over the person who can't read," Mark Twain wrote. Of course, *you* are not in this camp. You have made it this far, which says much about your determination to become well read. No matter where we are in our reading journey, we can improve, but it doesn't just happen. It takes a commitment, a plan, and a community.

How many times have I made my list of resolutions with gusto and determination on New Year's Day, only to forget what they were by the end of the month? Good intentions are not enough. For years, I wanted to read more and would say, "Oh, there is a long weekend coming up. I'll read then." And yet, again and again, I let my good intentions be sabotaged.

We can't wait for hours of reading time to come our way. Benjamin Franklin once said, "If you fail to plan, you are planning to fail." We need to be intentional, to make a plan and carry it out. Instead of saying, "One day I'll be a reader," let's say: "This is day one of becoming well read."

In this chapter, we offer strategies and tips to form your plan and overcome objections. We will show you how to develop a regular reading practice, improve your comprehension and retention ability, and identify six common mental obstacles that may be sabotaging your reading efforts. Onward!

DEVELOP A REGULAR READING PRACTICE

If you want to form the habit of reading, scheduling a short block of time into your daily schedule will help you make more headway than waiting for a weeklong vacation in the summer. Let's look at how this could be done. Set a goal. Schedule a block of reading time for yourself four to five days a week, if not daily. How?

Step 1: Look at your calendar.

Planning our weekly schedule is a common experience. We take a look at the upcoming week with its appointments, activities, and events and try to gauge the week and our plans. As you look over the calendar, remember to schedule routine self-care for your heart, mind, and soul. Ask yourself, "Where is there a window of time where I can read for twenty to thirty minutes?" Or ask, "What can I stop doing so I can read?"

Look for these times and mark your calendar (or set your phone alarm). Writing it down may be enough to help you remember; at 2 p.m., I will stop what I'm doing and pick up my book (which is waiting for me on the kitchen counter). Resolve to be faithful to honor this appointment with yourself. Maybe it's daily for twenty to thirty minutes, or maybe it's for longer periods on lighter days. It can even be for five or ten minutes at first. The idea is to establish regular reading times and get them written in your calendar.

Step 2: Show up for your appointment.

This second step is a bit more challenging. When I schedule a haircut, it's a commitment, and I show up. If a friend calls to try to get together, I look at my calendar and ask, "When else could we meet? I'm getting my hair cut then." If I can be faithful in a commitment to take care of my hair, I can honor an appointment to feed my heart, soul, and mind.

Step 3: Ask, "What do I want?" and plan accordingly.

Have you made a commitment to finish a book within a certain time, such as for a monthly book club meeting? How can you estimate how long a book will take to read all the way through, in the allotted time period?

Simple. Time your reading.

It doesn't matter if you're slow. It really doesn't. Take a book, even the one you are holding now, focus your attention, and time yourself as you read a full page. How long did it take you? Now multiply the number of minutes by the number of pages in the book to approximate how long it will take you to get through this book. Is it three hours? Is it eight and a half? It doesn't matter.

Now ask, "When do I hope to have this book finished? How much time will I need to allocate to finish by this time?" Next, look at your calendar. Do you see a couple of possible evenings or mornings where you could dive in more deeply to complete the book in the allotted time? Schedule those reading sessions in your calendar.

Step 4: Adjust your schedule—or expectations—as needed.

You can't find enough time in your schedule? Well, how much does completing the book mean to you? You may need to change your definition of success. If you aren't able to read a whole book a month, read what you can in the time planned.

One woman I know went to her book club for two years without finishing a single book. After two years, however, something changed. She began to finish the books ahead of her meeting time. Either her reading ability was improving or she found creative ways to work more reading into her days. Either way, by staying with it, she experienced success. If you're in a book club and you persevere in your daily ritual but don't get the book done, pat yourself on the back. You are establishing a lifelong habit.

Another woman I know chooses four or five selections a year to read and discuss with her book club (instead of the recommended ten), and she faithfully finishes these. Success looks different for everyone. So, leave the guilt behind and keep at it. Persevere.

No step is too small. Faithfulness to small steps builds momentum. With each little step, affirm your success. What you were able to read this week was something! Congratulate yourself. "Good job!" It was more than would have happened had you not sat down with a book at all. Make a plan for next week. Recommit to your plan and ask yourself four little words: "What do I want?" Then ask why.

TIPS TO HELP IMPROVE YOUR COMPREHENSION AND RETENTION

As we pointed out in earlier chapters, digital content has changed the way many of us read. It will take time to build up the discipline of focusing your attention on the printed page. That is to be expected. But don't give up. Over time, and with a few simple techniques, you will find that you gradually build up a sustained reading habit. Here are some of the strategies we have found most useful.

Ask yourself questions as you go.

The goal here is not to pass a test or write a paper; the goal is to get more enjoyment and enrichment from a book. When you are drawn to a particular line or image, mark it and write questions in the margin as you read—it helps to enhance your engagement.

Read summaries to stay on course.

It can be easy (and frustrating) when navigating through confused, complex plots and a multitude of characters in the story. There can be a great deal coming at you, especially in the first chapters of a novel. You're trying to get a handle on the author's writing style, the historical setting, the dialect, the plot, the characters, and who's related to whom.

I will often refer to CliffsNotes or other resources to familiarize myself as I go. Reading a chapter summary or character list can make it easier to stay on track and comprehend more quickly. The point here is to use resources to assist and ease you into the story.

Manage your attention.

Use a white index card to assist with linear (line by line) tracking. One of my children has a form of dyslexia, and his teacher encouraged him to place a white index card on the page and move it down line by line as he reads. It helped him to move his eyes from left to right. With so much scanning online, I keep a white index card in my novel and use it when I've been on the computer during the day. I don't use the card all the time, but especially when I am tired, it makes linear tracking and focus easier.

Read for five focused minutes.

If you have trouble staying focused, set yourself up for success with short five-minute bursts of attentive reading. If you know you only need to focus for five minutes and then you can take a break, it may be easier to manage your attention.

Use the inside back cover to create an index or chart.

My friend Tracey and I share books back and forth, and I am privy to how she marks her books. More than once, I've come across her indexing chart on the inside back cover. It is not complicated, but depending on the story and what she is interested in at the time, she may create a chart on the back that helps her be on the lookout for certain ways an author incorporated particular traits in a character.

For example, she may list virtues across the top: faith, hope, perseverance, patience, and so on. Then she draws lines horizontally and vertically, listing the names of the characters vertically on the left side of the chart. When she comes across a description of patience, she notes the page number in the box. You can index whatever topics are interesting or helpful for you. Here are some possible topics to index depending on the book:

📖 Virtues

📖 Signs of foreshadowing or turning points in the story

📖 Insights you gain through the various characters on friendship, faithfulness, work habits, and the like

Use color to mark your book.

I love to use colored highlighters, especially for more challenging works. It helps to keep me engaged. Here is one way to use color to highlight text:

- 📖 Blue—"beautiful." Highlight phrases of beautiful prose or powerful descriptions.
- 📖 Orange—vocabulary. When I encounter a word I don't know, I mark it in orange. Sometimes, just the process of taking the time to highlight the word helps me ask questions about the surrounding context to intuit the word's meaning.
- 📖 Yellow—idea! Certain paragraphs or sentences spark an idea or interesting concept. How did the author think of this? Is this how people thought about electricity (or whatever it is) in this time period? When I find a way of thinking fascinating or experience an "aha" moment, I highlight it with yellow.
- 📖 Green—"growth." Is there a phrase where a character shows moral growth? Maybe a timid soul becomes courageous. Or perhaps a vengeful person moves to a state of forgiveness. Is there a section that I want to ponder more for my own growth? I will highlight these parts in green.

Can't use highlighters? How about Post-its? If I am borrowing someone else's book, I use Post-it Notes (blue, orange, green, and yellow) and record my thoughts and questions on those instead. When finished with the story, you can put the sticky notes on paper with the name of the book at the top and save them in a binder.

READING HACKS TO SET YOU UP FOR SUCCESS

Are you finding it difficult to keep up your regular reading appointments, even after scheduling them dutifully on your calendar? Does your family seem to spring to life the moment you settle down in your reading chair? Here are a few hacks to help you sustain your reading habit.

Create a reading ritual and prepare in advance.

To motivate you to keep your appointment for regular leisure, a little preparation might do the trick. It did for me. When my kids were little, there was always work waiting. Always. There was laundry to fold, dinner to think of, the refrigerator to clean. I was desperate for some daily quiet, prayer, and a chance to read my novel.

So, especially in the winter months, I got in the habit of setting up an "afternoon reading tray" early each morning while the coffee was brewing. I placed a wicker tray on the kitchen counter along with tea, a little teapot, a tea cozy, my favorite mug, my Bible, notebook, current novel, pencil, a pretty napkin, and maybe some chocolates. The prepared tray sat on the table all morning, reminding me that in the afternoon a time of relaxation was coming my way.

It didn't always work, but with the books and teapot ready on the counter, there was one less hurdle to overcome to take that break in the afternoon. Instead of working through nap time to get more done, there was almost a sense of obligation to stop work for at least a few minutes and honor this earlier gift of preparation.

I remember many a winter afternoon, carrying the tray up to my room, pouring a cup of hot tea, taking a deep breath, and soaking in some quiet with the realization that I didn't have to push every moment. I could read, rest, and recover. These intentional rituals helped me sustain momentum for the long haul—and they will help you, too.

Have a place for your book.

It sounds so simple. But how many times have I been looking forward to getting back into the book I've been enjoying, only to discover it is nowhere to be found? While I am the type of person who has four to eight books going at a time, the one for the book club is the main one I need to keep in a designated place. I have spent many hours over the years searching for my novel. It seems it should be easy to keep it in a certain place, but this hasn't come naturally for me. Lately I've been keeping my current selection by the phone charger on our kitchen countertop. We'll see how it goes.

My daughter Beth struggles to keep track of her books, too. A week before her book club was meeting to discuss *Ida Elizabeth* by Sigrid Undset, she couldn't find her copy anywhere. She searched the car, under the beds, in the kids' rooms, and outside. Hmm, where in the world could it be? Two days before her meeting, Beth headed to the garage to take out some meat for dinner, opened the freezer, and there—sitting on top of the frozen hamburger—was *Ida Elizabeth*, the bookmark still in place! With a sigh of relief, Beth finished the novel minutes before her meeting.

Don't be afraid to start.

A retired woman in her seventies, Karen provided childcare at her parish so a group of young moms could take part in an hour-long book club once a month. After three years, the women decided to move their meetings to homes. So, when one of the women called Karen, she assumed they still needed help. "No, we have childcare covered. We want to know if *you* will be in our group."

Excited but a bit nervous, Karen began the first book, a thick novel by John Steinbeck. "Can I tackle something this challenging?" she wondered. "It's been quite a while since I last read a novel." As she started reading, she was alarmed to find she was not comprehending the story. So she started from the beginning again, and the same confusion happened again. She was unable to focus or comprehend.

Karen was saddened. "Oh, I so wanted to be in this group, but I guess I will have to tell them I don't have the attention span to read this kind of book anymore." But instead of giving up, she started again, for the third time, from the beginning. This time, she slowed her pace. She marked her book. She jotted notes in the margins. After three chapters, she told me, "Something clicked; I couldn't put the book down. I absolutely loved it."

She went to the discussion. "These young moms kept thanking me," Karen remembered with a laugh. "They said I brought a perspective that they needed. I think it's from living more life. I've faced a lot of challenges over the years."

Because of her willingness to go back and reread several times when she struggled to comprehend, Karen is experiencing friendship and enjoying literature. She had the humility to begin again, and we can too.

SIX MINDSETS TO AVOID

As with Karen, who had to really push herself to read and comprehend Steinbeck, the thought of stretching yourself to read and enjoy great and worthy books might be a bit intimidating. Before long, that little voice in your head whispers all sorts of excuses, reasons why you can't—just *can't*—make time for that now. (Or can you?)

Here are six of the most common excuses—and how you can overcome them (just as we did!).

Mindset #1: "I don't have time."

This is the number one reason many don't read. It implies that if we *did* have time, we would be sitting in our gliding backyard lawn chairs sipping iced tea and plugging our way through all 992 pages of *Don Quixote*.

"I don't have time" is the go-to line to assuage guilt and let ourselves off the hook. The truth may be that we do not feel we have the energy, stamina, or concentration to push through a challenging work of literature. But when this self-talk becomes a belief, our desire to read is sabotaged by the greater desire to continue living the way we are.

So the question is not "Do I have time?" The question is, rather, *"What is it I want?"* This question prompts me to consider how I want to live and to recognize a level of personal responsibility to bring this about. You may find yourself answering, "I am a creative person. I will find fifteen minutes today to read."

You seek out a time within your day to work reading in. It's working; you are reading. Slowly, you let yourself take in the text.

Your attention is focused and calm, and then, sure enough, another obstacle that can kill your motivation arises. It is called *distraction*.

Mindset #2: "I'm too distracted."

You have steeped your herbal tea, settled in with your cozy afghan, and opened your book to enjoy some relaxed reading time. Then, before you even finish the first page, urgent thoughts surface. As you reach for your tea, you glance up and spot a wayward gym sock. "Why is that sock on the floor?" Surprisingly, the sock becomes increasingly annoying. You can't concentrate. So you get up, take the sock to the laundry room, and while you're there, you switch clothes from the washer to the dryer and start another load.

Back on the couch, you settle in again, but before even finishing the next page, another problem presses urgently. "I need to call the dishwasher repairman back. I should do that now before I forget. Where is my phone?"

Getting up, you find your phone and call the repairperson. While setting up the appointment, you notice six zucchinis on the counter that really need to be used soon—actually, *tonight*. Before you know it, you're scrolling on Pinterest for zucchini recipes. Now your time for reading is over. The baby is up, and carpooling to soccer and piano begins. You're frustrated with your lack of focus. "Why does this happen when I sit down to read? Why do I get so distracted?" Could it be that distraction is not the root problem?

First, let's recognize what is happening. Are these thoughts about tasks you must take care of, or do they reflect a more fundamental challenge? Whenever you attempt to form a worthy, life-enhancing habit like reading, a disciplined prayer time, or an exercise routine, you will meet this challenge. It is a familiar enemy, and it's called *resistance*. By following one simple rule, you can counter this challenge: *Read first! For ten minutes.*

You can do anything for ten minutes. When you counter the temptation and focus, you experience success, and your routine is strengthened. Many times, when I use this tactic and read for ten minutes, I'm able to coax myself to continue just five minutes more. Sometimes, just five minutes more turns into fifteen or twenty extra minutes. And with this focused reading experience comes a sense of accomplishment. Here is the hack: Resist resistance by reading first.

Mindset #3: "I'll never get this done on time."

You may be right. You may only get part of the book read. Over the years in my book club, many women have not been able to finish the novel. Sometimes, it's because of life circumstances. Other times, it's because the woman's current reading ability is not at the level where it is possible to finish a book in the time that she has to dedicate to it.

The key is to affirm perseverance. Were you faithful to read regularly? Did you slow down? Did you comprehend what you read? Did you go back and reread when you needed to? Did you jot down notes about the characters and who is related to whom, especially at the beginning of the novel?

If you form the habit of regular reading, a little each day for ten to thirty minutes, you will make more headway in the long run than waiting for a weeklong vacation in the summer. Read what you can in the time you have. Don't feel guilty if you don't finish a book on time. Stay with it. Faithfulness and consistency over time will change your story. You are on the road to becoming a reader. Do not despise the day of small beginnings.

The time you spend reading is *something*. Affirm your success. See what happens next week. Review and recommit to your goals. Why do you want to become a reader? Take heart. As the process of focusing and comprehending gets easier, the enjoyment and relaxation will increase and it becomes easier to read more and read well.

Mindset #4: "What good is ten minutes when trying to read a novel hundreds of pages long?"

A ten-minute decision is a little step—and yet it is also a big step when it comes to becoming a reader. Little by little, we grow stronger and more capable. I tackled one of my all-time favorite books, Victor Hugo's *Les Misérables*, by using this ten-minute strategy multiple times throughout the day.

It happened this way. One day Beth called. "Mom, I don't see *Les Misérables* on this booklist you sent me for next year. I thought we were going to read that one."

"Beth, I know we were, but I got to thinking. The book is nearly a thousand pages, and we have a couple of other big novels next year, so I pulled it from the list. I thought it might be too much to ask of the women."

"Mom, are you serious? You agreed *not* to lower the bar. If we don't read *Les Misérables* in Well-Read Mom, when will we ever read it? I need my group to help me. Please, Mom, put it back on the list."

See the pressure I'm up against? So, back on the list it went, and when the time came to read Hugo's novel, I was leery. "Can I really tackle this long, old book?" I had my doubts. We had two months to read it, but for me, they were two extraordinarily busy months. My son was graduating, we had First Communions and end-of-the-school-year events going on.

Less than two weeks before my book club, I still had four hundred pages to go. Four hundred pages! Thinking back to Beth's urgency and the reason we put the book back on the list, I remembered her plea: "When will any of us read this great work of literature, if we don't help each other and read it together? If we are serious about becoming well read, this is a great book, and it has stood the test of time for a reason."

Ten days before my meeting, I stood in the grocery store parking lot commiserating with Janel, who had just pulled up. She listened as I carried on about all our family's commitments and how I wasn't getting much reading in.

"Well," she said matter-of-factly, "maybe this time you will have to say, 'I just can't do it.' Remember, there is only one rule in Well-Read Mom: if you don't get the book read, don't apologize."

"I know, Janel, but I lead this book club. I don't feel right not finishing it." I left the parking lot with a decision to make: "Do I finish the book or accept the one rule?"

Driving home, I asked myself, "What do I want?" I knew the answer. "I have always wanted to read this book, and I'm really enjoying it. If I don't finish it in the next ten days, will I ever? The time is now. I'm going to do my best to finish this great book."

Following this decision, as often happens, my creativity kicked in. I went home, and before I even unloaded the groceries on the counter, I found *Les Misérables*, set my kitchen timer for ten minutes, went outside on the back step, and read first. Ten minutes! Ding! I reset the time for ten minutes more! Ding! I got up, put the groceries away, and started dinner. Early in the evening, I was at it again, for ten minutes and again and again.

You can guess what happened in the following days. By staying at it, for ten determined minutes at a time, one hour before my book club discussion I finished one of the greatest novels of all time. With a sense of pride and accomplishment, I walked into Jill's house filled with gratitude. I think I gave every woman there a hug. I was grateful for these women in my little town who are journeying together toward what is good, beautiful, and true.

Thank you, Beth, for your insistence that we not lower the bar.

Do not despise small steps or small beginnings; they are a way to plant seeds of becoming well read. And one day, we will actually begin to find pleasure, leisure, and joy in the process. A sense of accomplishment follows every step we take to beat resistance and give space in our day for self-care.

Mindset #5: "I don't enjoy great books."

What if you desire to become a reader, but you don't enjoy great books? This might not be the reason why, but could it be possible that you are a fluent reader but not yet a deep reader?

When I was teaching high school students, I noticed students every year who didn't seem to enjoy the class as much as others did.

One year, two of the students didn't like the literature we read—at all. They sat bored. In a frank discussion with them, they told me they didn't like these kinds of books. They found them boring.

As we talked more, I realized that they were watching You-Tube summaries and scanning and skimming their way through the selections. They weren't slow-reading. Without engaging and comprehending the story, it's no wonder they found class boring. Although they had achieved fluency, they were not deep-reading. When it comes to enjoying great books, we must move from shallow to deep reading. There are no magic shortcuts. Time spent reading matters; there is no other way for the brain's neural circuitry to form.

Sometimes, it takes working our way through lots and lots of easier, familiar books before we move past fluency to a deeper understanding and engagement. In my class, I switched up my plan with these two students and read aloud with them as much as I could. I decreased the required number of pages and encouraged them to listen to recorded versions while following along in their book. I explained the goal was not the number of pages they got through. I asked them to slow down and read for ten minutes with focused attention several times a day. My hope for all the students I taught was for them to grow as readers and enjoy literature.

Many students today achieve a level of fluency but, sadly, not a level of deep reading. And they will miss out. If you feel this could be you, don't give up. Stay with it. It will take time for these deep-reading processes to be formed or re-established. Then, when they are, vigilance will be required to maintain your ability—but it is possible.[1]

Mindset #6: "I hardly remember anything I read."

Have you ever felt this way? I have. First, let me encourage you. Most of us don't have a photographic memory, and we will forget a great deal of the details in a novel. While there are helps listed in the next few pages to increase comprehension and retention skills, I want to encourage you there is more that happens in a great book than remembering the details. There are intangible, qualitative benefits to reading great books.

When failure thoughts like "You are not smart enough" or "You can't remember anything you just read" come rolling in, check yourself. Let those thoughts go. It could be you are reading in digital mode and need to slow down—way down—and switch to deep-reading mode.

Use strategies that work for you to increase your comprehension and increasingly relax and enjoy your book. If you need to refresh your memory before your discussion, read through a summary or your notes before the meeting. We are reading not for detailed memory recall but for enjoyment and transformation. So let those thoughts go and keep at it.

If you've made it all the way through this book this far, through chapter 6, you have some perseverance and motivation. Wherever you are in your reading journey, you are on the road and can say with growing confidence, "I am a reader, and I'm becoming well read." Try some of these strategies to overcome obstacles and gain momentum.

GETTING BACK ON TRACK

Home from college for the summer, my former student Elijah knocked on the door. I (Marcie) was just finishing cleaning up the kitchen after dinner and looking forward to putting my feet up to watch the NBA men's championship finals. After chatting for half an hour with Elijah, I asked him if he wanted to watch the game.

"No, I'm not into basketball, but go ahead."

"OK, if you don't mind, I'll mute the sound so we can keep talking. I just want to keep an eye on the score." Uncomfortably aware of how much I was into the playoff games, I tried to justify my viewing: "I don't usually follow the NBA."

"Me either. I'm not into pro basketball," Elijah went on. "I guess I'd rather spend my free time reading; I've read five novels since I got home a month ago."

"Five novels! You're kidding me? But aren't you working full time?"

"Yes, but not many of my friends are home this summer, so I'm using my free time to read. I love it."

I was caught off guard. Elijah *looks forward* to reading after work. Sure, he is single, and yes, it's true he is in a unique stage in life, but still, it takes a decision and an effort for him to use his free time this way.

As he shared, I understood that reading literature has become a source of pleasure and relaxation for him. But still, Elijah's reading habits went deeper. What seems an insurmountable hurdle for most of us—reading five novels in a month—is possible not just because of his state in life—which is definitely part of it—but also because he is in shape. He is fit. He reads strong! And Elijah is reaping the benefits of deep reading: stamina, insight, critical thinking, perspective, discretion, and intelligence.

I thought about how I had spent my free time over the past month. The playoffs started mid-May with the NBA East-Coast games, which led to tuning in to the alternating West-Coast game the following night. By game three, I was hooked, and before I knew it, I'd logged nearly twenty-one basketball games by mid-June.

I was a bit shocked to realize that I'd squandered fifty-plus hours glued to the screen (already forgetting which team played which in the earlier rounds). "Why have I given so much time to this? Here I am, leading a national reading organization, and yet I get off track so easily. Why is it almost automatic to turn the TV on at times, but it seems to require a Herculean effort to pick up a book?"

It is easy to get caught up in the lure of the next sporting event or barrage of available entertainment. Pete and I enjoyed watching the playoffs, but we agreed we must be mindful and intentional to help each other, not squander our time. As Epictetus once wrote, "You become what you give your attention to."[2]

Together, we can help each other focus our attention on a few great things: the purpose of life, our human brokenness, our need for redemption, and the reality of grace.

ACTION STEPS

- Take a personal inventory of how you spend your leisure time this week. Look at your calendar and highlight the blocks of unclaimed time. Then, in your journal, for one week write how those blocks were "spent." What do you notice?
- What are some of the negative mindsets that trouble you about your ability to read deeply and well? What is one thing you can do to put these thoughts to rest?
- If you could read one book—any book—from cover to cover, what would it be and why?

Ready to get started?

- *Turn. Off. Social. Media.* Put your phone on silent. Hang a sign on your door to discourage distractions. Tell yourself you'll only have to focus for ten to twenty minutes.

- *Keep a "to-do" list handy*, so if a task comes to mind, you can jot it down without going on your phone. Return to the book, return to the focus.

- *Set short goals, and reward yourself.* Set a short goal—such as reading every day for five days straight for ten to twenty minutes. If you are able to keep going, keep going. If not, you are faithful with your small step, and you can tell yourself, "Good job!" Don't forget to reward yourself, even just verbally. It can be as simple as "Good job" or "You did it." Don't underestimate this little affirmation. Success builds on success.

- *Narrate the story to yourself.* Are you having trouble finding focus? To increase comprehension, read out loud, then stop after a couple of paragraphs and share with yourself what is happening in the story. Something like "It seems there is tension between these two families, but I'm not sure why. I will look for clues as I go." Hearing yourself verbalize what you think is going on is another way to increase your comprehension.

- *Reread a few pages.* Having trouble jumping back into the story when you pick your book up again after a few days? Start by rereading the last few pages over again to "build momentum."

- *Set a reasonable goal.* Say, fifteen minutes a day to start. Use whatever time you have, and don't underestimate the importance of these minutes with a book, even if you only get through a few pages. At the end of the fifteen minutes, if you can, keep going.

Set a realistic goal and attain it. The experience of meeting even a short goal is a success; you will be encouraged to do it again.

Struggling with "reader's block"?

📖 *Read "even when . . ."* Rather than wait for inspiration to read, sit down and read the book "even when" it is not convenient. I like to say, "When you don't have time to read, work reading in." If you wait until you have an opportunity to lie in your hammock for two hours with no interruptions, you will be waiting a long, long time.

📖 *Stack your habits.* One good habit can lead to another, and it is easier for this to happen if we stack good habits. I'm trying to eat a healthy snack in the afternoon and drink more water. Eat the snack, then drink the water. They are both good habits; put them together, one after the other. How about stacking your reading habit this way? Brew the tea, and gather the book. Relax with the tea while reading the book.

📖 *Have an accountability partner.* Find someone who is at a similar life stage and has similar reading goals, and meet together to read. One Saturday a month my daughter Beth and her friend Annie go to a lake, sit on the sand, and read for half an hour before they allow themselves to visit.

Remember, it is not where you start that matters. By consistently persevering, you will become a better reader. Rather than waiting to find inspiration to read, find a little time to read each day. Keep showing up. Keep following the steps and strategies step-by-step, week by week. You are becoming a reader . . . and that is the first and most important step to cultivating the well-read life.

PART THREE

Reading to Enrich Your Soul

"To learn to read is to light a fire; every
syllable that is spelled out is a spark."
—Victor Hugo

Great books spark our imaginations, allowing our hearts to grow in empathy and love for the struggles we face this side of heaven. We need to activate our memories to hold on to our hard-won insights, so we can return to moments of desolation, growth, and consolation and see our story in the context of the larger narrative of which it is a part: "His"-story. Our lives are filled with characters, rising action, tensions and conflicts, climaxes, and resolutions. Then it starts all over again. Once we see this pattern, we can see how human stories participate in the divine story.

We are not alone in our search. Community is central to self-discovery. Christ gives meaning to our struggles and joys because he allows us to be grafted onto his own death and Resurrection, which gives the whole of life a definite shape and telos.

CHAPTER 7

Intentional
Journaling:
Make It Your Own

"Preserve your memories, keep them well,
what you forget you can never retell."
—Louisa May Alcott

Sometimes we don't know what we think until we shape our thoughts into words and arrange the words into sentences and paragraphs. The act of writing corrals vague impressions into specific reactions, interpretations, and insights. The very act of writing a question may spark an answer to that question. Writing also increases the likelihood that we'll remember a thought. This chapter offers a sampling of journaling styles for readers to consider, along with prompts to get them started. Intentional journaling also sets us up for meaningful discussions with others.

So you have decided to take steps to grow in your humanity by putting down your phone, reclaiming leisure, and feeding your imagination. You have received some concrete steps on how to choose great and worthy books and what to do with a book once you have cracked open the first page.

Now comes what is perhaps the most important step for our continued commitment to reading for pleasure, growth, and transformation . . . *remembering* what you have read and taking the time to record how you have been changed by your reading practice. Once you begin journaling, you will recall so much more of the hours you have invested in reading and have a record of the way these books have shaped you to pass on to your family and friends.

MY "JOURNAL JOURNEY" BEGINS

Back in 2019, I (Colleen) was reading *Middlemarch* by George Eliot. Our group decided we would meet to discuss it over two months as it was 794 pages long. As a slow reader, this was a daunting task for me. I arrived at my friend's house ready to discuss the book, and my friend Brenda was giddy with excitement. Her daughter's boyfriend had just flown in and was planning to propose to their daughter that evening.

As we sat sharing our impressions of *Middlemarch* and the varied types of marriages Eliot put on display for us to ruminate upon, art was reflecting life. We were talking about marriage as young people were about to find out about it for themselves. Each character in Middlemarch accompanied me on a journey of discovery, and the humble ending of this novel sneaked up on me and planted itself deep in my soul: "But the effect of her [Dorothea] being on those around her was incalculably diffusive: for the growing good of the world is partly dependent on unhistoric acts; and that things are not so ill with you and me as they might have been, is half owing to the number who lived faithfully a hidden life, and rest in unvisited tombs."[1]

Unhistoric acts. Hidden life.

Dorothea's life resonated with my own. This sounded like the kind of work I do every day—small things, hopefully done with love. Can our small acts of love and service really change the world?

My day progressed from book club in the morning to soccer try-outs in the afternoon to an event in the evening for my husband's employer. That evening they were honoring a former CEO who had been stricken with Parkinson's disease. As he stood up to wave to the employees for his recognition, I marveled at this beautiful man. He was one of the good ones! He worked hard, led the company with expertise and confidence, and cared just as much about giving back to the community as he did about financial success. The recognition of the fruits of one's labors at the twilight of life, followed by a concert and *joy*! It was one of those "rich" days when you feel as though you've lived a lifetime in one day.

The next morning, I looked at my iCalendar from the previous day, which listed my appointments in a series of lines between hours of the day. The "list" of appointments at prescribed times did not contain all I experienced that day! I made a resolve—without delay—to start journaling. I wanted to remember! To remember the conversation we had about marriage and *Middlemarch*; to recall my son's bounding around the soccer field awash in youthful glory; to hold on to the look of the retiree's eyes as they filled with tears in gratitude for a well-lived life.

But I had a problem. I was not the journaling type. As a mother of five with sparse free time to boot, I did not want my desire to become a "project" that I would abandon in time. When I went to look for a journal to give the right form to what I wanted to write, I was turned off by the journals I found. Many had a date on every page. The prospect of writing something every day felt like an albatross around my neck.

In the end, I experimented with various kinds of journals and, unsatisfied with them all, decided to design my own. It is called *Between the Lines*—a reference to the inadequacy of recording my days on the lines of my iCalendar. I did not want to feel like T. S. Eliot's character J. Alfred Prufrock, my life being "measured out in coffee spoons" but rather to see more in my daily life. Just like a good novel, to get the most out of a good book you must read *between the lines*. There are strands of gold in many of our daily encounters, if we have eyes to see them and the capacity to remember them.

I remembered how much I loved reading *The Secret Diary of Elisabeth Leseur*. Elisabeth Leseur was a "woman of the world," according to her husband, Felix. She spoke several languages and lived in Paris with her atheist husband, where she hosted dinner parties and met other social obligations appropriate to her position in life. In 1899, at the age of thirty-three, she secretly began writing her journal.

Elisabeth suffered many injustices living with a husband who not only did not share her faith but would often mock her religiosity, along with his friends. Felix repeatedly tried to persuade Elisabeth to reject the faith, but at age thirty-two she experienced a profound deepening of her faith. She decided to accept and embrace all her sufferings for the conversion of her husband. She began to journal, detailing how she took Felix's barbs against her beliefs and offered them in trust and silence to our Lord.

In 1914, Elisabeth died and left behind her journal hidden under her bed. Felix found the journal and began to read about her heroic love for him. One year later, Felix reconciled with the Church. In 1919, he entered the Dominican order and in 1923 was ordained to the priesthood. At Felix's urging, the Church began to investigate her cause for canonization. These proceedings seemed to die out with Felix's death in 1950, but in 1990 the Church reopened the cause for Elisabeth's canonization.

An atheist husband turned Catholic priest—all because of a journal! In 1917, Felix decided to publish the secret journal, and he later published other writings by Elisabeth that he had discovered. This collection was printed in English in a single volume as *The Secret Diary of Elisabeth Leseur*. I pulled down this book from my bookshelf and began paging through it for inspiration.

In the introduction, Felix writes, "Elisabeth's *Journal* is a history of a soul noting the principal stages of its evolution, a kind of examination of conscience set down by hand in odd moments. And as the author wrote for herself alone, this conscience disclosed itself to God in all simplicity, truth, and freedom, without a thought of style or of composition."[2]

These were words I needed to hear. Leseur had wanted just what I wanted: to write freely and quickly, noting the "stages of evolution." Leseur didn't write daily, just when she had something to say or record. Therefore, I decided my journal would not have a page dedicated to each day but instead a place where you could record the day. If you missed a day, there was no failing, no sense of waste—only pages to fill. Here is one of my favorite entries in Leseur's journal: "Let us open our hearts to admit all humanity. At the touch of the divine, let us resound with every generous thought, every human affection; let us learn to find in each soul the point at which it is still in touch with the Infinite, with God."[3]

I (Colleen) created the "Read between the Lines" journal to help the Well-Read Mom community capture and record their insights . . . and perhaps it will help you, too! You might like to get a copy through the Well-Read Mom website or create your own from a blank journal or notebook. *Between the Lines* is structured with the following prompts. (And we made it beautiful, with gold lettering and a linen cover, because your life is beautiful, and it matters.)

Date/day of the week.

As I have already mentioned, Leseur wrote when she was struck by something or wanted to record something profound. She was often silent about the "unhistoric acts" of each day. I find this inspiring, for my good intentions to write are frequently thwarted by life: a child or elderly family member comes down with the flu and needs care; the roof leaks and you are left sopping up the mess. Keep your journal handy—by your bed or in your purse—and write when something emerges that you just don't want to forget. This isn't social media—no need to post regularly or stage beautiful images like you do on Instagram. It's your life—the more you offer, the more you get into the habit of noticing, the more you will see. The more you write, the more you will remember.

Intentions of the day.

In the Catholic tradition, there is a long-standing practice of offering your "works, joys, and sufferings" of the day as a spiritual gift on behalf of or for the intention of someone else (like the Holy Father's monthly intentions). You are uniting your "works, joys, and sufferings" to Christ's sacrifice of the Mass as an intercession for someone else. This is called the Morning Offering.

There are many versions of this prayer, but I like this one from St. Thérèse of Lisieux the best:

> Oh my God! I offer You all my actions of this day for the intentions and for the glory of the Sacred Heart of Jesus. I desire to sanctify every beat of my heart, my every thought, my simplest works, by uniting them to His infinite merits; and I wish to make reparation for my sins by casting them in the furnace of His merciful love.
>
> Oh my God! I ask of You for myself and for those dear to me the grace to fulfill perfectly Your holy will, to accept for love of You the joys and sorrows of this passing life, so that we may one day be united together in Heaven for all eternity. Amen.[4]

Intentionally offering my joys and sufferings for another has changed the way I approach each day. Each moment is a gift that can be used for the sanctification of someone else. It has been a blessing to reread past entries, looking over my days and remembering the people who have asked for prayers. There are so many people and situations needing prayer today. There is so much weighing heavy on my heart. Write it down. Record it. Maybe the solution to your problem will become clearer as you write your prayers. If you would like a special journal for this purpose, pick up a copy of *The Ave Prayer Intentions Journal* (Ave Maria Press).

Poignant moments/follow-up thoughts.

This section can be anything you want it to be: a reminder of things to get done, a brief note about a conversation you had with a friend, a letter you received. I remember a conversation with a dear friend who took me out for lunch when I was going through a particularly rough time in my family. She spoke three phrases that would change my life. She told me *"to accept, to surrender, and to embrace"* my sufferings.

When I got to my car, I wrote those three words down on a scrap of paper, and I added them to my journal when I got home later that night. It amazes me how looking back on that day, years later now, floods me with memories of love and genuine friendship. What she said that day made my sufferings easier to endure. How easily those powerful words could have been lost had I not taken a moment to solidify them. Keep it short—get right to the "gold" of your day.

> "Actually, paper is more advanced and useful compared to electronic documents because paper contains more one-of-a-kind information for stronger memory recall."
> —*Kuniyoshi L. Sakai, University of Tokyo*[5]

What brought me joy?

Depression and anxiety are on the rise and taking an enormous toll on our population. Science shows that if you can focus on gratitude and joy, it improves mental and spiritual health. In this section, record what made you smile each day. Record something beautiful you saw. Your teenager gave you a hug unexpectedly. Your husband cleaned up the dishes. You heard a great song on the radio and belted it out for only you to hear. In short, what moved you today?

When Marcie and I were just getting to know each other, she shared with me how often days would pass by without feeling like she was really connecting with her children. She reflected on how to change this dynamic; she decided to take some Post-it notes and write these reminders to herself all over the house:

1. Look each child in the eye each day.
2. Delight in each child each day.
3. Laugh with each child each day.

I took this wisdom to heart, and my own connection with my children has grown and deepened as I have tried to live more joyfully and intentionally with my children.

Struggles and shortcomings.

We know failure can be a powerful teacher. We grow through our struggles and learn grit and perseverance. For me, it is difficult to name these areas in my own life and face them honestly, because it exposes the truth that I am not perfect or in control of my own life. However, by writing down your struggles, you can witness your transformation over time. When a person suffers, they often think it will have no end. When we live through our sufferings, we see how they give rise to new life and that pain doesn't last forever. As the French poet Léon Bloy said, "There are places in the heart that do not yet exist; suffering enters to bring them into existence."[6]

A few years ago, my friend Samantha was going through a tough time. Samantha felt disconnected from her children as they dealt with the struggles of being teens. It was heart-wrenching for her to live with this chasm between parent and child. Samantha's mother suggested she buy a notebook and write "letters" to her children to unburden her heart. It was cathartic for her to get out frustrations, hurts, anger, and hopes for her children in a truthful way. Later, Samantha confided in me that writing these letters helped her to look at herself with clearer eyes and discern what she could change to love her children more effectively. Writing helps process emotions, invites reflection, and provides an opportunity for transformation.

A quote to remember.

Everyone needs some inspiration each day! In the *Between the Lines* journal, I compiled quotations from the first ten years of the Well-Read Mom's reading list. These quotations helped me to reconnect with books I had read with my group. A rich quote from a master work can help the experience of reading that work come alive again. These quotes reinforce the reading journey I began years ago by reminding me of beautiful insights to live by.

What I am currently reading.

Record the book(s) you are reading. I have often thought how interesting it would be if we had a record of everything one of our favorite authors or saints read. If we track ours, perhaps we'll see a pattern to what we are reading, the kinds of ideas we are thinking about, and the ways our hearts have expanded through literature and the events of our daily lives.

Lessons learned (favorite quotes/character/events).

Reading literature helps us to grow in our humanity. In this section, make a connection between the literature you are reading and your own life by interiorizing some aspect of the novel. This habit will make getting together to discuss the book more enjoyable, because you have been applying the themes to your own life.

Today I am grateful for . . .

As Georges Bernanos wrote in *Diary of a Country Priest*, "Grace is everywhere." How easy it is to live distracted and small! Gratitude reorients us to infinite Love—it enlarges us.

During a particularly dire day, I wrote in my journal that I was grateful for "air." I remember the day vividly. Truly, not being able to produce one single thing for which I was grateful, the only thing I could come up with was air. I am glad I was honest and did not just put something down that was not in my heart. However, I look back to that challenging time in my life and see how it has passed. The rain did stop. Greener pastures emerged. But that entry is a consolation to me, because so many prayers were answered! God stooped to help me at my lowest point (so far). There will be other struggles, there will be dark days ahead, but I have proof that God is good and remains faithful to me.

Gratitude helps so many facets of our lives. According to Robert A. Emmons, a leading expert on gratitude, professor of psychology at the University of California, Davis, and founding editor-in-chief of *The Journal of Positive Psychology*, there are many ways gratitude helps us to live fuller lives. Here are some of the scientifically-proven benefits of cultivating a meaningful habit of gratitude.[7]

Gratitude helps to

- Enhance spirituality
- Make us happier
- Improve sleep
- Lower blood pressure
- Prevent overeating
- Increase energy
- Strengthen immune system
- Improve pain tolerance
- Control glucose
- Extend life span
- Reduce inflammation
- Boost self-confidence
- Improve patience
- Reduce envy
- Improve optimism
- Aid in addiction recovery
- Enhance vitality and sex drive
- Manage grief
- Remember events in a more positive light
- Improve retention, productivity, and decision-making skills
- Build better relationships
- Increase generosity
- Reduce materialism

A few years ago, while I was in spiritual direction with a Jesuit friend of mine, I was complaining that God seemed very abstract to me. He recommended I add the Examen prayer to my nightly routine and be sure to end my prayer by listing three things I was grateful to God for each day. My friend said to be sure to name these gifts *as coming from God*—that is the key. "Thank you, God, for the beautiful sunset tonight with my husband. Thank you, God, for the successful surgery. Thank you, God, for your Word and for speaking to my heart in the scriptures."

As soon as I began this practice, God was no longer remote but moving through the experiences of my life. If we choose to see even the smallest things as gifts from God, we will be able to see him operating in our lives more each day.

> "Do not be anxious about anything,
> but in everything by prayer and
> supplication with thanksgiving let your
> requests be made known to God."
>
> —*Philippians 4:6*

Book summary.

In the last twenty pages of the journal, there is a section to record each book you read, a brief description of the characters and the plot, the page numbers of your favorite quotes, and what you want to remember about the book.

It is incredible, when I reread my *Between the Lines* journal, how much more I remember when I take five to ten minutes at the end of a novel to cement my experience. If we take the proposal of reading quality literature seriously, we are going to devote hours of our week to this encounter. Why not take a few extra minutes to make sure you are going to remember what you read?

The connection becomes *written in memory* and provides a tangible record of what books moved me and what I took away from them. Who knows? Perhaps one day my granddaughter or grandson will discover it. Maybe she will be curious to read alongside the figures from the past and be encouraged as I whisper in her ear what beauty, goodness, and truth there is to behold in this mysterious world.

ACTION STEPS

📖 Purchase a journal and set it in an area where you will see it daily (in the car, by a favorite chair, on your nightstand). I keep a small notebook in my purse, and if something strikes me during the day, I jot it down in the moment and transfer it to my journal at night. (Be sure to check out the *Between the Lines* journal at https://wellreadmom.com).

📖 As you become more habituated with marking your books, reflect on a line you highlighted or underlined—use that as a prompt for your writing.

📖 Start with the prayer intentions and the gratitude prompts for a few days to get in the habit of writing; then fill in the rest as you are drawn.

📖 When you finish a book, take time to flip to the end of the journal and record your thoughts on it with page numbers of favorite quotes. Reread this section every year.

CHAPTER 8

Connect with Other
Readers

"It was books that taught me that the things
that tormented me most were the very things
that connected me with all the people who
were alive, who had ever been alive."
—James Baldwin

Because each person is unique, our experience of a particular book is different from anyone else's; therefore, we have something personal to share with other readers, and they with us. This reciprocal fellowship enriches our experience of literature and life by weaving beautiful threads of understanding among us, uniting disparate parts and synthesizing our human experience. These threads of understanding and unity reach beyond the people discussing and serve to strengthen the community at large. When women thrive, their families and communities thrive.

*R*eading and discussing literature together can be a simple yet powerful way to build social connections that are necessary for spiritual growth, good mental health, and personal happiness. In the years that I have been involved in the Well-Read Mom movement, we have worked to distill our method into key steps. This four-step process enables us to make the most of our reading practice.

- 📖 *Read.* Give yourself time and permission. Banish guilt!
- 📖 *Compare.* Use your imagination to apply what is happening in the book to your own life.
- 📖 *Share.* Get together in person (preferably) to discover new insights.
- 📖 *Accompany.* Keep these books alive by staying together with your friends and helping them in their lives.

By following these steps, you will gradually acquire the skills and capacities to become truly "well read"—to be able to process, comprehend, reflect deeply on great literature, and enrich your relationships with the insights you have gleaned from that investment of time and effort.

"Wait," you may be thinking. "When I think of working my way through a hefty novel, I see myself even more isolated from others. How can reading help me build relationships?"

It sounds paradoxical, but more than twenty years of personal experience have shown me: sharing books is a shortcut to friendship.

READING FOR FRIENDSHIP

My (Marcie's) daughter, Margaret, was in sixth grade when Well-Read Mom began. She knew that Beth, Steph, Aunt Janel, and I were working together on some kind of book club. Without paying much attention, Margaret went about her business doing all the things a twelve-year-old girl likes to do. Meanwhile, the grassroots group started to grow, and so did the workload. Soon, running this little initiative began to involve Margaret and the whole family. In the early years, the kids pitched in to mail out hundreds of reading companions.

Margaret reflects, "Even when we were stuffing piles of packets, I didn't think much about what was happening in this book club. It wasn't until women started coming up to me at church and other places sharing their gratitude for Well-Read Mom that I became aware: Something special is going on here. Reading books together is making a difference in these women's lives.

"When I left home for college, I began to experience my own version of loneliness. Sure, I had friends at school, but we were in different classes, and what dominated our talk was all the work we had to do. 'How can I stay with my friends in more meaningful ways?' I asked myself. 'We need a shared experience.'

"I asked my mom if there were any extra reading companions and then proposed the idea of reading three or four of the selections throughout the school year to a small group of my classmates. That's how, as a single college student, I got started. Now, post-college, the group continues, and so do the friendships! This experience has fostered a depth of relationship I needed. For me, it has been a shortcut to friendship."

When you come together having read the same book, the shared experience begins. The individual time and effort spent focusing one's attention on a novel bring astonishing payoffs. Meaningful dialogue is an experience of community.

Whenever we get together, we are not showing up for shallow chitchat. We gather, having *thought about* something. From this starting point, we dive into discussion. When you have *something interesting to talk about*, you have a springboard for thoughtful conversation and a catalyst for one of the most human and humanizing activities we can partake in—conversation.

Sharing the same story, the same month, even if—or especially if—it's a challenging one, brings a sense of satisfaction. Add a few insightful questions, personal experiences, and a bit of vulnerability, and presto, friendships form. Honest dialogue, even when we disagree, builds connection among us. My friend Linda calls our book discussions "sacred time." She is right.

Where do you desire to have more meaningful connections? In the relationship with your husband, your teens, the women in your parish, your coworkers? It is possible. Take a risk and propose a book to read and discuss together. Or ask one other friend if she would join you. You may be surprised to see what happens.

Stories of a Well-Read Life
When Following Is Freedom

I have been blessed, truly blessed, to have been a small part of Well-Read Mom (WRM) since its infancy. When I was a brand-new mother, I met with Marcie in a little rundown café to talk about a new idea she had. I was instantly intrigued by what she called "Well-Read Mom," because, although I had only been a mother for about three months at the time, I was already feeling the stagnation that constant conversation about diapers, baby milestones, and play dough recipes can bring. When WRM began, I was all in. Hooked. I jumped into my group headfirst and read each book with excitement. Which is why it may seem odd that last year I intentionally gave up reading a single Well-Read Mom book.

I don't really know what drove me to make the decision to abandon WRM's booklist. Perhaps I was feeling like a rebel. Or I just wanted to have complete control over at least one thing. I just remember telling my group that I would still come to meetings for the snacks and the laughs, but that I was going to read whatever the hell I wanted. You see, I don't have a problem with picking up a book. In fact, some might say I've been known to ignore my children from time to time in order to read just "one more page" (I'm not saying I'm proud of it). At first, it was great. I was reading what I wanted, when I wanted, and just indulging myself.

As with every decision, there are consequences. Of course, it was still lovely to attend my group meetings. I could sip tea and nibble on the best of treats . . . but I was noticing how much less satisfying it was when I could not participate more deeply in the discussion, when I could not contribute anything that could tie in to the book that was being discussed.

An unforeseen consequence, however, was that I began to notice the unique and beautiful gift of each of the women in my group in a new way. I noticed how each one grappled with tough themes. I noticed their differing viewpoints on a variety of subjects. I was moved to see their hearts laid bare when they earnestly dove into the work that was being proposed and that they were willing to share that bared heart with *me*! I guess that if I had read every book, I may not have shut up enough to be able to notice these things about my fellow readers. About halfway through the year, I also began to notice that I was sad to finish a book of my own choosing and not have anyone to sit down and share it with. Needless to say, once spring rolled around, I was happy to be back on the wagon (just in time to hang out with Kate in *East of Eden*!).

We are a lonely culture, a culture that values "being rebellious" over true, deep happiness and fulfillment. It's kind of baked into the cake at this point, and I've found myself having to consciously decondition from this "self-reliant" mentality. Really, it all boils down to pride, yes? But truly, I need people. I always have and always will need people—and there is a true freedom in following something that has been proposed in love. This year, I have read each book with diligence. Not every book chosen has been my favorite, but I have judged *all* of them to have been a boon for my daily life and worthy to have been read and discussed. I am grateful to Marcie for this invitation to lay down my weapons of self-destruction.

As Bernard Berenson put it so eloquently, "Literature in its most comprehensive sense is the autobiography of humanity." I believe this to be true, and, if this *is* true, it makes my emotionally driven philosophy of last year silly, albeit educational. Sharing literature within a community has been a more profound experience of freedom than being a rebel has ever been. Now, excuse me, I must get back to reading Brother Lawrence, who, strangely enough, is speaking of community, dependence, and freedom . . . four hundred years ago! Happy reading, sisters.
—Susan Severson

READ TO BUILD RELATIONSHIPS WITH OLDER CHILDREN

A woman from Indiana approached me (Marcie) at a gathering: "This is my first year reading with all of you in the book club."

Curious, I asked, "Have you noticed any changes in your life because of it?"

She pondered. "Hmm, well, I would have to say my relationship with my fourteen-year-old daughter has improved."

This surprised me. "Really? That's wonderful. Which book helped you the most with your daughter?"

She paused. "I don't think it was any one book; it was reading *these kinds* of books and discussing them in my group that has helped. I am able to see her perspective on things in a new way. It is hard to explain, but my daughter and I are talking again."

What strikes me about this mother is that by disciplining herself to read the selections she most likely wouldn't have chosen on her own, her relationship with her daughter is improving. Rather than creating greater distance, the time spent reading has widened her perspective, which in turn is narrowing a gap in their communication. Engaging with a variety of literature opened a door for understanding and brought about a change in her way of being with her daughter.

A similar thing happened to me, but in a different way. When my son John was in high school, he sometimes got up in the middle of the night scavenging for something to eat. One night, around 2 a.m., John sat eating a bowl of cereal in the living room. Eyeing St. Augustine's *Confessions* on the bookshelf, he "took and read." The next morning, I found the book (and the cereal bowl) still on the kitchen counter and was curious: "John, were you reading St. Augustine last night?"

"Yeah, I was hungry and couldn't sleep. Mom, have you read this?" he asked, holding up *Confessions*. "It's pretty good! You should check it out."

That's how our discussion of St. Augustine's dramatic conversion began. I was aware of the tremendous gift of this conversation in John's life and mine. And it came about because years earlier, I read this classic with my friends. This book, in our home, on our shelf, stood waiting for John when he was restless and hungry, eating a bowl of cereal at 2 a.m.

Becoming well read is like planting seeds that suddenly spring to life at unexpected times. More meaningful connections with our children, our husbands, and in all our relationships are possible and may surprise us how and when they come about. Meaningful relationships down the road come from the intentional decisions we make today.

ACCOUNTABILITY MATTERS

Another way that regularly sharing books counters loneliness and enhances connection is by providing a secret weapon: accountability. With a time and a place to meet scheduled right into your monthly calendar, something kicks in—creativity to get the job done.

When it comes to reading, I finish a novel not because I'm such a good reader or even because I like it. Almost every single month, it's because I don't want to let my friends down. What I can't seem to do with willpower, for my own good (read a great book once a month), I will do with regularity because of my friends.

Accountability with friends is a win-win: we are helped to be faithful on the reading journey, and being faithful to the reading, in turn, strengthens meaningful connections and builds a social life, a regular and protected opportunity to reveal our innermost thoughts.

Why is this important? Let me give you just one example. Some time ago I ran into a friend who was going through some hard things and clearly needed to talk. The next day I called to see about getting together, and together we began to look through our calendars.

"Would Monday morning work?" I asked.

"No, I work. How about Monday evening?" she proposed. "Oh, never mind. The boys have basketball, and Megan has dance."

I persisted. "Could you meet on Wednesday?"

"No, I help with CCD, then there is children's choir practice."

Thursday, Friday, and Saturday were also out. Our juggling continued another five minutes, just trying to find a forty-five-minute window of time to share a bit of heart-to-heart conversation. Finally, we decided to call each other in two weeks and start this unsatisfying process of finding a time to meet all over again.

By building regular meeting times into our schedules, in advance, there's no more phone tag! When a monthly time is on the calendar, we know we will see our friends. If we just show up month after month, friendships form . . . and miracles happen.

PROTECT SACRED TIME

Not long ago, I asked the women in my book club if they would mind if we all left our phones by the front door instead of within arm's reach around the circle of chairs. Linda was the first to reply: "This is a good idea. I am not offended by you asking this. We need to protect this time. It's sacred time."

Another woman chimed in, "Guarding against technology needs to be a team effort. Let's help each other protect this hour and fifteen minutes together."

Just then, my phone, which was by my side, buzzed. Here I was, the one who had just suggested no phones, impulsively eyeing the text message. I apologized to the ladies, but after checking my phone, I noticed a subtle change descend over our group. The momentary distraction had shifted our train of thought.

That night, I understood something true for my life. What I need to "not miss out on" is *not* a text message. I need to protect myself from missing out on the gift of "sacred time." Now, to honor my friends and myself, I leave my phone at the door.

HOW TO START A GROUP

When you have a regular group you meet with on a set day and time each month, it's easier to build the rest of your life around it.

Sometimes, these "standing appointments" (like waiting in a carpool or outside the parish classrooms) might even be opportunities to *start* these regular connections. Since you know you'll be there anyway, why not make that time meaningful? Why not start a group?

It all begins by taking a risk. I (Marcie) remember the day in the fall of 2012. Gripping twenty-two postcards in my hand, I was on my way to the post office on Main Street to mail the very first Well-Read Mom invitations my daughter-in-law Stephanie had designed:

> *What*: Well-Read Mom: A book club where we will read great books, worthy books, and spiritual classics together.
>
> *When*: September 12, 2012.
>
> *Where*: Marcie Stokman's living room.

Clinging to the twenty-two invites, I stood with my arm up to my elbow in the blue mailbox. Now I had a problem. I couldn't let go. As I stook there, paralyzed by fear, thoughts of failure whirled in my head. "If I drop these, this idea becomes real. Who do I think I am to start a book club where I give the introduction? I'm not an expert. No one does this. This is nonsense. They'll think I'm crazy."

In that moment of profound doubt, where did I get the audacity to drop the invites? What helped me take the risk?

I asked myself a difficult question, one that would ignite courage and move me to action. I asked, "What do I want?"

And then I answered my own question: "I want to read, and I need accountability. I want meaningful conversation and friendships. I want to grow and live a beautiful life."

Then that answer segued into prayer: "Lord, I want to love you more, and I don't know why, but reading literature helps me in my relationship with you."

The postcards were still clutched in my hand, so I tried a dose of reality. "These books weren't written for experts; they were written for ordinary people like me. Most women aren't reading, and neither am I."

My desire rose. The postcards dropped. Well-Read Mom began. Looking back, I was seeking to grow in my relationship with the Lord and with my friends. I was looking for face-to-face conversation, intellectual stimulation, and fun.

THREE KEYS TO RECLAIMING TIME

I've come to understand three things about reclaiming time to read and grow in friendships:

1. The decisions I make (or don't make) matter.
2. I have more control over how I spend my time than I often realize.
3. Accountability with friends encourages me to make better choices.

Living a beautiful life requires time and discernment. We have choices to make, and as the years go by, choices, even little ones, make a difference in our quality of life.

Jeff Olson and John David Mann wrote, "The truth is, what you do matters. What you do today matters. What you do everyday matters. Successful people just do the things that seem to make no difference in the act of doing them and they do them over and over and over until the compound effect kicks in."[1]

To recover time to connect with others, look at how you are spending your days and then, with courage and intentionality, make the changes you need.

READ, COMPARE, SHARE, ACCOMPANY

By reading, we mean giving ourselves *guilt-free* permission to find space and time (during the good hours of our day!) to read selected literature, allowing it to penetrate our hearts and minds. This will entail slowing down, reclaiming leisure, ordering our time, and adjusting our priorities. These efforts will be rewarded by greater connection and meaning.

Read Slowly and Savor the Experience

A few weeks ago, my friend Sadie called me. "Colleen, I just can't read these books. I just don't think I'm smart enough. I've started the same page several times, and I just don't get it."

"Sadie, how many books have you read this week?"

"Three! That's what's so crazy! I'm a fast reader."

"Can you tell me how these books struck you?"

Silence. Then she added, "I've forgotten most of them by the time I pick up the next book."

Now, Sadie was an avid reader, but different books make different demands on us. Sadie was reading as a *consumer* versus reading as a *seeker.* When we read to gulp down a plot hastily, awaiting the next action, we are conditioning our brain to treat books as another product to consume. We should not seek satiation but rather transformation. Reading to discover our humanity and to be awakened to *meaning* requires an alternative starting point: watchful attention. Being aware of this dynamic is half the battle.

I encouraged Sadie to read during her best hours of the day—even if it is over a lunch break or twenty minutes in the morning. Enjoy. Savor the words—and go slow. The more she reads in this unhurried way, the more she will retain. These books are not for academics. They are for us! I encouraged Sadie to ask herself, "What meaning is offered in this story? And what does that have to do with my life?"

This is the spiritual work we are doing when we compare great literature to our lives. It is analogous to an examination of conscience: What are we doing? How have we loved? How have we failed? What are we seeing? What places in our hearts do we avoid? The more we cultivate introspection, the more our conversations will be deep and bear fruit. When people read in this way, much will be shared and discovered. We will grow.

Compare the Story to Your Own Life

Comparing is the step where we make what is happening in the story applicable to our own lives. As we read, we engage our imagination to bring the scenes and characters to life, but imagination does not stop there. Imagination is the meaning-making faculty of the intellect that helps us translate the words and actions of characters into experiences that have the power to change us. We distill the universal meaning from the particular circumstances of someone else's life. This step is essential from bringing the story from our head to our heart. This step is easy to overlook if you just read for the action of the plot, but deep, transformative reading entails an education of the entire person: head, heart, and soul.

STORIES OF A WELL-READ LIFE
Charis Changed My Life

I normally journal on planes, but I didn't this time; I couldn't bear to look at my nagging, aching heart just then. Instead, I decided to read a book that had captured my attention: Marly Youmans's *Charis in the World of Wonders*.

Charis has a deep heart and she listens attentively to its joys, sorrows, aches, and concerns. And as Charis spoke about herself and her life throughout the book, it placed me right in front of my own heart. Her words echoed in the part of my heart that continually cries out for more, and I felt God using the lines of the book to draw me to himself. I began writing my thoughts in the margins, even though I didn't want to journal.

"There are times I wish I could scream away my desire for more," I wrote. "I cannot. But if I did, what would it cost? I could gain the whole world and lose myself."

Before this plane ride, I had wrestled with whether to break up with the best boyfriend I ever had—a kind man, a good man, a man who is pure, holy, a gentleman, and a hard worker. I had journaled and journaled and journaled but was stuck. I was stuck because I was afraid.

Yet there on that plane, Charis's heroic attention to her own heart gave me courage to listen to mine. "Truth and sorrow were better companions than happy lies," she said. I knew I had to make a change. Some have criticized the plot for being a fairytale; too simple and predictable. But fairytales have a particular ability to witness to something, in G. K. Chesterton's words, "more mystical than darkness and stronger than strong fear."[2] I am grateful to Charis, who helped me know my heart—and not only know it but follow it courageously.—Teresa Petruccelli

SHARE THE EXPERIENCES OF THOSE UNLIKE ME

Reading *The Autobiography of Miss Jane Pittman* was an awakening for one woman I know. Although a fictional account of a life (despite what the title suggests), we were introduced to the African

American experience in our country in a new way through this novel. One woman shared her story:

"Of course, I have seen destitute, poor people panhandling before. My usual response is not to give them any money and to walk past without making eye contact. But for some reason after reading this book, when my family went on a recent vacation to Miami and I saw a Black man with a cup out on the corner, I bent down and really looked in his eyes. I handed up twenty dollars and asked his name. There was something I recognized in his eyes, something we shared."

Reading *The Autobiography of Miss Jane Pittman*, this woman found herself asking a painful question: How do I treat others of a different race than my own? By walking in the fictional shoes of Miss Jane—a slave in bondage, an emancipated person fleeing a powerful oppressor, a sharecropper, a hired hand, and an advocate for justice—we can see how long the struggle for racial equity has been. We feel different because the struggle has a face, a name. My friend took a step in living differently. This is the beginning of personal transformation. This is the beginning of cultural change.

Accompany in Discovery

We are not meant to exist in isolation; our nature is fulfilled by living in community. Long ago, Dorothy Day understood, "I was lonely, deadly lonely. And I was to find out then, as I found out so many times, over and over again, that women especially are social beings, who are not content with just husband and family, but must have a community, a group, an exchange with others. Young and old, even in the busiest years of our lives, we women especially are victims of the long loneliness."[3]

Meeting to share books becomes one way to counter loneliness. In this work, we come to know we are not alone. Literature has been called the "autobiography of humanity." When questions arise in our hearts, and someone else understands what we are asking or recognizes themselves in an experience you share, you see that this hidden part of yourself—the part you maybe thought was yours alone to bear—is, in fact, hidden deep in *every* human heart. This becomes an experience of communion.

But what if I don't have anything to contribute? What if I don't have questions that arise, or what if I'm the slowest reader in the group? Well, what if you are the slowest one and what if you don't have much to say?

I think back to when my boys were in cross-country. My son, Philip, was the slowest runner on the team. The small but determined, well-coached group of nine runners from our town won sections and then went on to place fifth in the state high school meet. Since only eight of the nine could take part in the state race, we were surprised to find that Coach Twigg had included Phil, the slowest runner on the team, on the roster.

Later, when I asked Coach Twigg how he came to this decision, he said something like this: "Phil has been a key factor for our success all season. Every day, he shows up and does his best. Everyone is better when Phil's around. He may be the slowest runner, but he is a key leader on this team."

Suddenly, I realized Philip played a role I hadn't considered. It wasn't as much about his speed and athletic talent as it was about his person and presence. This played a part in forging the team's spirit and success.

You may doubt your abilities. You may be the slowest reader in your group, and you may think you don't have anything of significance to contribute. You are mistaken. Reading what you can, showing up consistently, listening with attentive focus, and sharing what you've thought about play a more important role than you may realize. Your presence, month by month and book by book, will contribute to culture-building.

Consider the little groups scattered across the country, all reading great and worthy books. You may wonder, "What can I do to make a difference in the world?" When we join together to read, each of us tosses a pebble in the pond, confident that a ripple will follow from each one of us. What is the ripple that follows? It is the change in us, hearts that soften and enlarge, increased human formation, an experience of community, conversation, and ongoing personal conversion. All of this will make a difference in the world.

One of the ripple effects we have seen in Well-Read Mom is that when women decide to read more, men decide to read more too. When women regularly bring quality literature into the home and set an example of reading for pleasure and for personal and spiritual growth, this work ripples out to the entire family. I know when I (Colleen) come home from a Well-Read Mom book club eager to share insights from my friends, my husband and children want to experience this depth, too. In just the last five months, my husband and son have read *Dracula* and *True Grit*, something that probably would not have happened if I were not in this group. Last week we sat down at the dinner table to discuss whether Mattie Ross in *True Grit* was seeking justice or vengeance for her father's death. We discussed ideas like justice, law, mercy, and grit because these characters were enfleshed in a way that was both artistically captivating and profoundly human. These conversations are essential to the education and nourishment of the mind, heart, and soul. And we shared a deeper experience that we can draw upon when a situation warrants it. How beautiful to share these deeper stories as part of our shared lexicon.

Stories of a Well-Read Life
A Story of *Two Old Women*

I remember when we read Velma Wallis's *Two Old Women*, a story based on Athabascan Indians of the upper Yukon River Valley in Alaska. In this legend two old women, who have been known to complain more than contribute, are abandoned by their tribe during a brutal winter famine.

As they stand together, frightened and stranded, death seems imminent to them. But with unimaginable courage, they resolve that if they are going to die, they will die trying. They get to work. They don't die, and in the process, they play a part in saving their people that winter.

What each of us would like to do is change the world. Together, we resolve not to complain, but to contribute. By becoming well read, we play a part in changing the world. Together we are taking back reading and raising the cultural conversation. My friend Susan Severson said it best when she once told me, "If we are going to fail, let's fail upward." I agree with Susan. Let's not stay where we are. Let's raise the bar. Let's become well read, and let's do it together.

Being accompanied in life is essential for human flourishing. Aristotle said two elements must be present for true friendship to exist: mutual goodwill and a shared common life. Becoming well read is not about amassing knowledge or discovering our

cultural heritage in literature, but most importantly it is a trans-
formational experience. Great literature helps us see the good,
the true, and the beautiful. We hope this search leads us to the
author of the whole of creation, God himself. Our stories are part
of a larger story—the story Christ has written into our hearts.
—MS

THE WAY OF HAPPINESS

St. John Paul II said,

> It is Jesus you seek when you dream of happiness; he is wait-
> ing for you when nothing else you find satisfies you; he is the
> beauty to which you are so attracted; it is he who provokes
> you with that thirst for fullness that will not let you settle for
> compromise; it is he who urges you to shed the masks of a
> false life; it is he who reads in your hearts your most genuine
> choices, the choices that others try to stifle. It is Jesus who
> stirs in you the desire to do something great with your lives,
> the will to follow an ideal, the refusal to allow yourselves to
> be grounded down by mediocrity, the courage to commit
> yourselves humbly and patiently to improving yourselves and
> society, making the world more human and more fraternal.[4]

Making the world more human and fraternal is one goal of becoming well read. When Christ instituted the Eucharist at the Last
Supper, he offered his Body and Blood, which would become present in ordinary bread and wine, to feed us sacramentally with his
very life. He knew it would be both a memorial of his death and
Resurrection *and* a meal, a place of community. Ordinary things
bearing extraordinary grace. While literature is not equivalent to
the Bread of Life, it does bear echoes of the author of creation,

because it deals with the humanity that Christ humbled himself to become one with.

Dostoevsky famously said, "Beauty will save the world."[5] But beauty does not save anyone; Christ does. Yet, when art is beautiful it can be a bridge to the religious experience. Transformation is possible only when something greater is offered. Jesus became a human person at the moment of the Incarnation. Time is measured by the Incarnation. This changes the way we understand the story of our life and the time we have been given.

> "The hint half-guessed, the gift half-understood is Incarnation."
>
> —T. S. Eliot, "The Dry Salvages"[6]

ACTION STEPS

- Take a step to join a book club. At Well-Read Mom (www.well-readmom.com) you can find a community of women near you by searching under the map feature on the website. Still unable to find a group? Email us at info@wellreadmom.com and we'll help you!
- Find an accountability partner. List three people you could share a book with and establish a discussion time to mark on your calendar.
- Set a daily routine to give some of your freshest hours of the day to reading, and stick with it.
- Actively spend three to five minutes using your imagination after you read to connect with the characters through exercising your empathic capacity.

Connect
Your Story
to the Larger Story

"We are not writing our own stories,
the Heavenly Father is."
—Fr. Stephen Gadberry

"There is something in us, as storytellers and as listeners
to stories, that demands the redemptive act, that demands
that what falls at least be offered the chance to be restored."
—Flannery O'Connor

As creatures made in the image and likeness of God, we are in a never-ending discourse with our Creator, whether we are reading scripture or choosing to invest our time and resources in contemplating the work of artisans. As we make connections between these works of literary imagination, we recognize in them components of a Grand Story—the overarching narrative of all reality, of which we are a part. My life, your life, the lives of our neighbors—reading well offers us a wider perspective that enables us to see God's design and embrace our part in it.

Every story has a beginning, a middle, and an end. If we turn our gaze to the scriptures, we see in them a very special story—the archetype of all story—because it tells the story of God from the beginning of creation to his promised Second Coming. God inspired human writers to communicate the "Grand Story"—the story of creation, loss, death, redemption, struggle, and the promise of a return. What would we know about God had he not chosen specific men throughout history to write down what he had chosen to reveal? This is a startling fact to wonder upon. What we know of God is handed down (tradition) through *the inspired storytelling of men.*

God created *ex nihilo*, out of nothing. He began an elaborate calling of things into existence through his word: "God said, 'Let there be . . .' And it was so" (Gn 1). The highest point of his creation is the making of man. "Then God said, 'Let us make man in our image, after our likeness'" (Gn 1:26). Through the speech of God, everything came into being, and everything created bears the stamp of his personhood, including his generosity. That is why everything that is created is good—it bears the trace of God. Man, however, was *very good*, because we alone were endowed with reason (*logos*) and human beings alone can respond to God with thought and free will (intentionality) and imitate him through procreative generosity. When we "make" things—be it children, as the highest expression of human love, or art—we are imitating the Maker. We are imitating his nature and responding to a primordial urge to know God.

The first four chapters of Genesis contain worlds to meditate upon. Everything that exists has been created. We were *given* both a garden in which to live in harmony and fruitfulness and a command to obey our Father in freedom. Would we trust him? We were tempted and we fell from our original unity and grace. Toil, pain, and death entered the world. A Savior was foreshadowed. As we untethered ourselves from God, our sins grew exponentially—from grasping at power in the serpent's promise of being gods ourselves (the apple) to murder (Cain and Abel) in one generation. All the stories written since Genesis have contained elements of this Grand Story.

St. John Henry Newman said, "Literature, as such, no matter of what nation, is the science or history, partly and at best of the natural man, partly of man in rebellion."[1] Literature is the study of man, of all that he has experienced since the beginning. So why should we read it? Why should we relive the pain of our separation from God? Because it is the best preparation for our own lives!

As Joshua Hren says (summarizing Fr. William F. Lynch), "Christ descended and passed *through* the particular in order to redeem. This movement is a model for the Christic imagination: the poet or fiction writer needs to pass through the concrete (the way down) in order to arrive at insight (the way up)."[2] We can study our own lives by looking at the "rebellion" in others and hopefully, through careful examination and grace, we can encounter the One who can save.

Back to Genesis . . .

In Genesis 2:18 there is one thing in the garden that is *not* good: "It is not good that the man should be alone." We know that today, more than ever, an epidemic of loneliness plagues our country. God knew it was not good for man to be alone from the beginning. We need friends! We need helpers who can point the way to God in the tangle of this world.

PILGRIMS ON THE WAY

Several years ago, Well-Read Mom chose "pilgrim" to be the theme for our reading year. Every book we read that year dealt with pilgrimage or journeying in some capacity. We decided at the end of the year to offer an actual pilgrimage for the women—a place where they could carry what is in their hearts in silence and prayer and concretely connect their life to the larger story that is being written for us by Christ. We read *about* pilgrimage and then we offered the chance to be *transformed* by one. We were connecting our story and grafting it onto the story God has been writing from the beginning of time.

We spent two and a half days walking. We took turns leading the group by carrying a processional cross, walking single file and often in sacred silence. We prayed for each other's intentions and felt buoyed by the unity growing in our group. We became true sisters on the journey. We saw miracles take place in our midst—healings manifested and prayers answered. It is astonishing to hear the "still, small voice" of God when you finally have a minute to enter more deeply into the world, paradoxically by leaving it for a few days. Our minutes, hours, and days were given over to understanding who God is and who we are. Each woman brought real intentions, many of them born of pain, loss, and grief, offering them to Christ step-by-step. From a few women in 2019, our numbers have grown each year, carrying the stories of our lives to lay at the foot of Mary in the place where miracles still happen. This has been a profound experience of accompaniment. The women stay together in prayer, silence, penance, and joy to help each other carry the struggles of our families collectively to Jesus through Mary.

We trust that Jesus will come again to "wipe away tears from all faces" (Is 25:8) and establish his justice forever. We will stand before him to account for the life we have lived. Deeply examining your life now in preparation for that final encounter is why Well-Read Mom exists.

Stories told in great literature are microcosms (or components) of the Grand Story—the overarching narrative of all reality, from Genesis to Revelation. And my life and your life and the lives of our neighbors—these, too, are significant parts of the whole history of the world. Each person is integral, each person has a story to tell. Reading offers us a wider perspective that enables us to see the whole and embrace our own part in it with a greater awareness of the sacredness of life, and to help each other obtain our true goal.

ONE LAST STORY ON FAITH AND FORMATION

In 2012, I (Colleen) was working as a director of adult formation for two parishes in the Archdiocese of Milwaukee. I saw Mass attendance beginning to dwindle and parish participation becoming more anemic. In 2002 when we joined the parish, most Masses had standing room only, but in the ten years we had been parishioners, the pews that were once full became sparse. Fewer people came to church, and those who did come often left early and were less engaged. I struggled to recruit volunteers to fulfill the mission of the parish, like being RCIA sponsors or leading prayer groups. Our parish, like many others, needed to become alive to why we need Christ. We needed to be awakened to rediscover the Church. We needed to experience the *meaning* of the Incarnation in every aspect of our lives. But how?

In times of crisis, the Church leans on artists and thinkers to re-pro-
pose the Christian message to a new generation. The Church bets on
culture as the way to shape hearts. I longed for more people in the
parish to have a common language, to discover the profound meaning of their vocation as mothers and fathers, and to dive into the
ancient wisdom of the Church as a rock to center us in the rapidly
changing (and often hostile) modern culture that was and is upon us.

And so I proposed we begin to read together as a parish community. We began simply by reading some of the great works of
the Western tradition together and discussing them. We paired
older parishioners with middle/high schoolers to read Dante's *Divine Comedy.* We asked Cistercian monks to come and share their
insights with us by meditating on St. Teresa of Ávila's *The Interior
Castle.* We invited people to read articles related to art, faith, and
culture and meet in each other's homes to discuss them over a simple soup dinner. People were engaged and started coming back to
the Church. Questions were being asked and taken seriously, and
deeper conversation began to take shape.

We decided our next "culture builder" would be to read a short
story by Flannery O'Connor and meet in the parish grove to discuss it. I searched for a presenter to come and speak on O'Connor,
and Marcie Stokman's name appeared on the other end of that
Google search. Somehow, I found her phone number and called to
invite her to present to our parish. She told me she had just started
Well-Read Mom and could not accept any outside engagements.
We talked for nearly two hours. When I hung up the phone, I
knew I had found a kindred spirit, a friend who shared the same
desire I had for meaning and friendship. She invited me to start a

WRM group and write for the yearly companion WRM publishes, but it was late in the summer and the parish schedule was already set. Still, I kept Well-Read Mom in my heart and kept ruminating on the invitation.

A year later, with the growing needs of our family, I decided to return to being a full-time stay-at-home mom. I knew I wanted to start a WRM group to continue the culture-building that had begun in our community. Marcie and I had not spoken in over a year, but I decided to attend the fall WRM conference in Minnesota. I asked my sister to attend with me, with some of our older teenage girls, as the conference was offering a breakout session for high schoolers to discuss Nathaniel Hawthorne's *The Birthmark*. As any parent knows, getting away for a weekend and leaving behind eleven children between us was no easy feat, but our husbands encouraged us to attend. We decided to even go a day early so we wouldn't be late, as we were driving up from Milwaukee.

We were having a relaxing afternoon, trying on hats at a local resale shop, when my niece got a call from a friend who was also attending the conference. "Elena, aren't you coming to the WRM conference?" Elena replied, "Yes, we are going and are so excited to see you tomorrow." The friend replied, "The conference is today, and they are about ready to start the last presentation." I had the wrong date! We flew out of the store, drove to the conference, and arrived in time to hear half of the last talk. Afterward, I went to the bathroom and burst into tears.

Someone saw me and told Marcie, "There is this woman crying in the bathroom. You might want to check on her." So Marcie went to find me, and I explained how bad I felt about getting the date wrong. Marcie looked at me and said, "It's OK, Colleen, we'll just bring the conference to you. My daughter and daughter-in-law are the presenters, and we'll find a time to give the whole talk to your new Milwaukee group."

At that moment, a friendship was born. Marcie had seen the needs of my heart, and she kept her promise. A few weeks later, Beth Nelson, Stephanie Stokman, and Marcie came to Milwaukee and presented to our group. Afterward, Marcie came to my home and we talked for three hours in my living room. I began collaborating with WRM immediately, and the next year, for the theme of the "Year of the Friend," we chose the artwork of Ernesto Gutierrez for the cover of the Well-Read Mom companion. This piece depicts a group of indigenous women with children strapped on their backs, walking together and looking at the horizon, while one woman looks directly at the viewer.

This piece of art hangs in my living room, where it is a reminder of our shared desires for depth and cultural renewal and serves as witness to where our friendship took root. Marcie and I had begun a journey together. We didn't know where it was going to take us, but we knew we wanted to follow Christ through reading literature and meditating on the human condition.

It is easy to let the demands of life pile up and to stop reading. It is also easy not to invest in friendship because of the "busyness" of everyday life, but finding greater meaning in one's life requires a *shared, lived experience*, because we are not created to find meaning in isolation but in *communion*. By crying in the bathroom that fall afternoon, I exposed a vulnerability I didn't even know I had—I needed friendship in a deeper way! Opening our hearts to others, exposing our need for accompaniment, allows the light to flow in. Friends help us to see ourselves more clearly and buoy us along our pilgrim way.

The friendship that began by a simple phone call has expanded to sharing our lives together. Our husbands and children have become friends. We have supported each other through our children's struggles, through the death of parents and loved ones, and encouraged each other to grow in our relationship with Christ. We are living proof that being accompanied through life changes you. It matters! Living a well-read life begins with a choice to follow a desire (to grow), is strengthened through friendship, and expands outward to build culture from the inside out.

BECOMING A CULTURE WARRIOR

As soon as World War II was over, leaving a wake of destruction across Europe, Communism entered the scene, posing dangers to human freedom as grave as the threats that had come from Hitler. A young Karol Wojtyla (later St. John Paul II) cofounded the Rhapsodic Theater with his theatrical mentor and friend, Mieczyslaw Kotlarczyk. The young Wojtyla knew preserving Polish culture (and the great works of poetry, literature, and drama) was the best resistance to the ideology of the day. So, young people would gather secretly, on pain of imprisonment and death, to practice and rehearse the works of their literary masters. They needed to keep the human story alive.

Today we find ourselves at a similar crossroads, confronted by many ideologies and technological forces, such as AI and quantum computing. We need to preserve culture and take back the arts from the demiurges that threaten to refashion it. Reading together is work, but it is worthwhile work, and it will bear fruit. Becoming well read involves coming to know more deeply who we are and the story of which we are a part. We have a deep-down need to hear the story of our family, our nation, our God. Through reading, we come to understand that we're part of a larger story, His-story.

A FEW LAST THOUGHTS TO INSPIRE YOU

You've done it! You've almost reached the end of this book and have discovered for yourself how to cultivate a well-read life. You understand that this comes with a price, and that there are no shortcuts. A life well lived doesn't come by allowing social currents to float us downstream; it requires a bit of resistance. By shutting the door on the ever-increasing tsunami of information and opening intentionally and consistently to pages of wisdom, we grow and learn and seek and find.

Join us on the journey to becoming well read. It's a simple proposal: "Let's accompany one another to read really good books." I'd like to officially invite you to join us—nearly ten thousand friends strong—to read more and read well, so you too can have a well-read life. And with that one life, you can change the world . . . starting with your own.

> "If my account of our moral condition is correct, we ought also to conclude that for some time now we too have reached that turning point. What matters at this stage is the construction of local forms of community within which civility and the intellectual and moral life can be sustained through the new dark ages which are already upon us."
>
> —ALASDAIR MACINTYRE, AFTER VIRTUE[3]

"The hour is coming, in fact has come, when the vocation of women is being acknowledged in its fullness, the hour at which women acquire in the world an influence, an effect and a power never hitherto achieved. That is why, at this moment, when the human race is undergoing so deep a transformation, women imbued with the spirit of the Gospel can do much to aid humanity in not failing."

—*St. John Paul II, Mulieris Dignitatem (On the Dignity and Vocation of Women)*[4]

ACTION STEPS

Take a moment to journal your responses to these questions.

- What does it mean to you to have a "Well-Read Life"? What do you want? How do you want to grow this next year?
- What are some of the most noticeable roadblocks to achieving this goal, and how do you plan to overcome these obstacles?
- What is one way to connect your story to the "larger story"? What is one thing you can do to take an incremental step toward that goal this week?
- Want to jump-start your reading and journaling practice? Visit https://wellreadmom.com/wellreadlife/ for bonus resources.

Acknowledgments

When I (Marcie) was invited to write a book for Ave Maria Press, my first reaction was excitement; my second, which followed immediately, was fear, a paralyzing fear. For me, writing a book is like scaling Mount Everest: you don't go it alone.

A friend once shared, "Everything good happens through friendship." I agree. So, in front of this worthy, but daunting, ascent, I asked (begged) Colleen Hutt to scale this mountain with me. She affirmingly agreed, and because of this *The Well-Read Life* is a much better book. Thank you, Colleen, for saying yes to yet another adventure. You know the meaning of grit, and together the journey becomes a joy.

We would like to acknowledge the incredible team at Well-Read Mom, especially Nicole Bugnacki, Janel Lewandowski, Mary Teck, Carla Galdo, Charity Hill, and Catherine Lacerte. We share in this work to grow in our humanity, to raise the intellectual bar, to nurture friendship, and to elevate the cultural conversation. You embody the feminine genius and make this work a true joy of the heart.

Thank you, Marcie, for asking me (Colleen) to accompany you in the life-giving work of Well-Read Mom. Our friendship began providentially ten years ago when I missed the Well-Read Mom conference and you offered to bring the conference to me, revealing the incredible generosity animating your life. I know this generosity has its wellspring in Christ, and your friendship has been the biggest surprise and gift of my later adult life. It is an honor and a joy to share in the work of Well-Read Mom with you.

I am forever grateful to my parents, Tom and Anne Wamser, for providing a liberal arts education, cultivating wonder, and teaching me the value of hard work. To my sister, Jennifer Deslongchamps, thank you for teaching me to ask the right questions and for awakening in me a love of great books. Your witness to the truth changed my life, and your ongoing friendship beautifies it. Bill and Martha Hutt, thank you for witnessing true hospitality and teaching me how any occasion can be elevated into an experience of beauty.

There are many people in my life who embody an ardent desire for holiness—continually seeking truth and pouring themselves out in love. I look to you with admiration and inspiration. I owe a particular debt of gratitude to D. C. and Jeanne Schindler, Stella Schindler, Joshua and Brittney Hren, John and Maggie Haigh, and Wendell Berry.

Thank you to all the women who follow the Well-Read Mom movement. We would like to acknowledge, in particular, the "original" Crosby/St. Paul groups and the Milwaukee/Oconomowoc women. Thank you for the life-giving friendship you have offered these many years. To the women who have inspired the stories in these pages—Susan Severson, Lydia LoCoco, Moira Moede, Kate Meyer, Jane Fee, Jen Deslongchamps, Anne Wamser, Ruth Pavelchik, Carrie Eck, Anna Malin, and Tammy Traub—thank you for sharing life with us, taking these books to heart, and being willing to share how you are being transformed through them.

This book would not have happened without the invitation and direction of Heidi Saxton, our editor. Thank you for gathering our ideas and helping to organize them into a systematic whole. You believed in us from the beginning and continually offered your insight, support, and friendship.

A special thanks to Dominic Hutt for hours of tech support. You were always patient and available when we needed you.

Notes

Introduction

1. Jessica Hooten Wilson, "Building Culture: How Reading Literature Educates the Imagination" (lecture, Women at the Crossroads of Culture: Well-Read Mom Tenth Anniversary Conference, Eagan, MN, January 29, 2022).

1. The Way We Read Is Changing

1. Naomi Baron, *How We Read Now: Strategic Choices for Print, Screen, and Audio* (New York: Oxford University Press, 2021), 6.

2. Marshall McLuhan, *Understanding Media: The Extensions of Man* (1964; repr., Cambridge, MA: MIT Press, 1994), 9.

3. Farhad Manjoo, "You Won't Finish This Article," *Slate*, June 6, 2013, https://slate.com/technology/2013/06/how-people-read-online-why-you-wont-finish-this-article.html.

4. "Eye Tracking: All the Secrets Revealed!," Waalaxy, January 9, 2023, https://blog.waalaxy.com/en/eye-tracking-ux/.

5. R. Buckminster Fuller, *Critical Path* (New York: St. Martin's, 1981).

6. David Russell Schilling, "Knowledge Doubling Every 12 Months, Soon to Be 12 Hours," Industry Tap, April 19, 2013, https://www.industrytap.com/knowledge-doubling-every-12-months-soon-to-be-every-12-hours/3950.

7. Sven Birkerts, *The Gutenberg Elegies: The Fate of Reading in an Electronic Age* (Winchester, MA: Faber and Faber, 1994), 256.

8. Dorothy Day, *The Long Loneliness* (New York: Harper and Row, 1952), 24–25.

9. Caryll Houselander, *The Reed of God* (Notre Dame, IN: Ave Maria, 2020), 26.

10. N. K. Sandars, *The Epic of Gilgamesh* (New York: Penguin Putnam, 1973), 85.

11. Aristotle, *Metaphysics*, in *The Basic Works of Aristotle*, vol. 1, edited by Richard McKoen (New York: Random House, 1941), 690.

12. Aristotle, *Metaphysics*, 690.

13. Robert Barron, "Why the Liberal Arts Matter," *Word on Fire Show*, April 10, 2023, https://www.wordonfire.org/videos/wordonfire-show/episode381/.

14. Charles Dickens, *Hard Times* (New York: Barnes and Noble Classics, 2004), 9.

15. T. S. Eliot, "The Dry Salvages," *Four Quartets*, accessed February 14, 2024, http://www.davidgorman.com/4quartets/3-salvages.htm.

16. Julian Kwasniewski, "John Senior: Prophet of Tradition and Realism," OnePeterFive, April 25, 2023, https://onepeterfive.com/john-senior-prophet-of-tradition-and-realism/.

17. Dante Alighieri, *Inferno* (Palatine, IL: Anchor Books, 2002), canto 1.

18. L. M. Montgomery, *Anne of Green Gables* (Urbana, IL: Project Gutenberg, 2008), chapter 18. Retrieved March 14, 2024, from https://www.gutenberg.org/cache/epub/45/pg45-images.html.

2. The Way We Relate to Others Is Changing

1. "Factoids," Bowling Alone (by Robert D. Putnam), bowlingalone.com, accessed February 14, 2024.

2. Douglas Nemecek, "Loneliness and the Workplace: 2020 US Report," Cigna, January 2020, 4.

3. Vivek H. Murthy, *Our Epidemic of Loneliness and Isolation: The U.S. Surgeon General's Advisory on the Healing Effects of Social Connection and Community*, US Public Health Service, Office of the US Surgeon General, 2023, 4, https://www.hhs.gov/sites/default/files/surgeon-general-social-connection-advisory.pdf.

4. Murthy, *Our Epidemic of Loneliness and Isolation*, 4.

5. Jamie Friedlander Serrano, "Experts Can't Agree on How Much Screen Time Is Too Much for Adults," *Time*, May 9, 2022, https://time.com/6174510/how-much-screen-time-is-too-much/.

6. Vivek Murthy, *Social Media and Youth Mental Health: The U.S. Surgeon General's Advisory*, US Public Health Service, Office of the US Surgeon General, 2023, 4, https://www.hhs.gov/sites/default/files/sg-youth-mental-health-social-media-advisory.pdf.

7. D. C. Schindler, "Social Media Is Hate Speech: A Platonic Reflection on Contemporary Misology," *Humanum Review*, September 17, 2020, https://humanumreview.com/articles/social-media-is-hate-speech.

8. *Phaedrus*, in *Plato: The Collected Dialogues* (Princeton, NJ: Princeton University Press, 1961), 523.

9. Schindler, "Social Media Is Hate Speech."

10. Wendell Berry, *Hannah Coulter* (Berkeley, CA: Counterpoint, 2004), 51.

11. George MacDonald, quoted in Kirsten Jeffrey Johnson, "Sacred Story," *Christianity Today*, October 8, 2016, https://www.christianitytoday.com/history/issues/issue-86/sacred-story.html.

12. Ole Edvart Rölvaag, *Giants in the Earth: A Saga of the Prairie* (New York: Harper and Brothers, 1927), 316–317.

3. An Armchair Revolution: Take Back Your Time

1. John Paul II, "Letter of Pope John Paul II to Women," June 29, 1995, no. 4, emphasis added, Holy See, https://www.vatican.va/content/john-paul-ii/en/letters/1995/documents/hf_jp-ii_let_29061995_women.html.

2. Josef Pieper, *Leisure: The Basis of Culture*, trans. Alexander Dru (San Francisco: Ignatius Press, 2009).

3. John Paul II, "Letter of His Holiness Pope John Paul II to Artists," April 4, 1999, no. 1, Holy See, https://www.vatican.va/content/john-paul-ii/en/letters/1999/documents/hf_jp-ii_let_23041999_artists.html.

4. Pieper, *Leisure: The Basis of Culture*, 46, emphasis added.

5. Pieper, *Leisure: The Basis of Culture*, 46–47.

4. Engaging a Story with the Head, Heart, and Imagination

1. Aristotle, *Metaphysics*, 25–28.

2. Maryanne Wolf, *Reader Come Home* (New York: Harper, 2018), chapter 3.

3. Vigen Guroian, "Awakening the Moral Imagination: Teaching Virtues through Fairy Tales," *Intercollegiate Review* (Fall 1996), reprinted at Catholic Education Resource Center, https://www.catholiceducation.org/en/culture/art/awakening-the-moral-imagination-teaching-virtues-through-fairy-tales.html.

4. Myron Magnet, "What Use Is Literature?," *City Journal* (Summer 2003), https://www.city-journal.org/article/what-use-is-literature.

5. Andy Murphy, "The Message Carl Jung Wanted the World to Understand," Medium, January 19, 2024, https://medium.com/change-your-mind/the-message-carl-jung-wanted-the-world-to-understand-e53f528531c0.

6. Holly Ordway, *Tales of Faith: A Guide to Sharing the Gospel through Literature* (Parkridge, IL: Word on Fire Press, 2022), 12–13.

7. C. S. Lewis, *An Experiment in Criticism* (London: Cambridge University Press, 1961), 13.

5. Choosing Books That Change Us

1. Guroian, "Awakening the Moral Imagination."

2. Dorothy Day, *The Duty of Delight: The Diaries of Dorothy Day*, edited by Robert Ellsberg (Milwaukee: Marquette University Press, 2008), 65, emphasis added.

3. Louise Cowan, "The Necessity of the Classics," read by Ken Myers (Charlottesville, VA: Mars Hill Audio Reprints, 2006), audio ed., 35 min.

4. Amy Lowell, "Poetry, Imagination and Education," *North American Review* 206, no. 744 (November 1917): 762.

5. There are many higher-education institutions that also have core curriculum or mandatory courses to provide a common literary and philosophical foundation, such as the University of Dallas, Ave Maria University, Franciscan University of Steubenville, Wyoming Catholic College, Belmont Abbey College, and Hillsdale College, to name but a few.

6. Carla Galdo and Colleen Hutt, "What Are the Criteria for Well-Read Mom Books?," *Reclaim Time for Books and Friendship, Take Care of Your Heart: An Invitation from Well-Read Mom* (Well-Read Mom, 2019), 9.

7. Pope Francis, "Address to Participants in the Conference Promoted by 'La Civiltá Cattolica' and Georgetown University," Vatican City, May 27, 2023, Holy See, https://www.vatican.va/content/francesco/en/speeches/2023/may/documents/20230527-convegno.html.

8. Lorraine Hansberry, *A Raisin in the Sun* (New York: Vintage Press, 1994), 145.

9. G. K. Chesterton, *Orthodoxy* (San Francisco: Ignatius Press, 1995), 52.

10. Willa Cather, *Shadows on the Rock* (London: First Vintage Classics Edition, 1995), 124.

11. Flannery O'Connor, *Mystery and Manners: Occasional Prose*, 1st ed. (New York: Farrar, Straus and Giroux, 1970), 96.

12. John Paul II, "Letter to Artists," no. 1.

13. Quoted in Jeffery A. Tucker, "Oscar Wilde, Roman Catholic," *Crisis* 19, no. 1 (April 2001), reprinted at Catholic Education Resource Center, https://www.catholiceducation.org/en/culture/literature/oscar-wilde-roman-catholic.html.

14. Luigi Giussani, *The Risk of Education: Discovering Our Ultimate Destiny* (Chicago: McGill-Queens University Press, 2019), 63.

15. John Steinbeck, *Journal of a Novel* (New York: Viking Press, 1969), 48.

16. John Steinbeck, *East of Eden* (New York: Penguin, 2002), 301. The actual Hebrew word is *timshol*, which Steinbeck renders as *timshel* in the novel.

17. Flannery O'Connor, *The Habit of Being: Letters of Flannery O'Connor* (New York: Farrar, Straus and Giroux, 1979), 354.

18. Steinbeck, *East of Eden*, 293.

6. I Have a Book . . . Now What?!

1. We believe it's worthwhile to regain or experience this ability, and we'll help you get there. Bonus materials can be found at www.wellreadmom.com/wellreadlife, or write us at info@becomingwellread.com.

2. Epictetus, *The Art of Living: The Classical Manual on Virtue, Happiness, and Effectiveness* (San Francisco: HarperOne, 2007), 52.

7. Intentional Journaling: Make It Your Own

1. George Eliot, *Middlemarch: A Study of Provincial Life* (Boston: Little, Brown and Company, 1905), 841.

2. Felix Leseur, introduction to *The Secret Diary of Elizabeth Leseur: The Woman Whose Goodness Changed Her Husband from Atheist to Priest* (Manchester, NH: Sophia, 2002), xv.

3. Elisabeth Leseur, *The Secret Diary of Elisabeth Leseur*, 16.

4. "A Morning Offering by St Therese de Lisieux," Beauty-SoAncient, October 3, 2023, https://www.beautysoancient.com/a-morning-offering-by-st-therese-de-lisieux/.

5. Kuniyoshi L. Sakai, *Frontiers in Behavioral Neuroscience*, as quoted in "Study Shows Stronger Brain Activity after Writing on Paper than on Tablet or Smartphone," Science Daily, March 19, 2021, https://www.sciencedaily.com/releases/2021/03/210319080820.htm.

6. Quoted in Fr. Patrick Briscoe, OP, "A Reminder of Good Things to Come," Aleteia, December 4, 2020, https://aleteia.org/2020/12/04/a-reminder-of-the-good-things-to-come/.

7. Robert Emmons, "Why Gratitude Is Good," *Greater Good Magazine*, November 16, 2010, https://greatergood.berkeley.edu/article/item/why_gratitude_is_good; Summer Allen, *The Science of Gratitude* (Berkeley, CA: Greater Good Science Center at UC Berkeley, 2018).

8. Connect with Other Readers

1. Jeff Olson and John David Mann, *The Slight Edge: Turning Simple Disciplines into Massive Success and Happiness* (Austin, TX: Greenleaf Book Group, 2013), 58.

2. G. K. Chesterton, *Tremendous Trifles*, chap. 17, https://ccel.org/ccel/chesterton/trifles/trifles.xix.html.

3. Dorothy Day, *The Long Loneliness* (New York: Harper and Row, 1952), 157–158.

4. John Paul II, "Address of the Holy Father John Paul II," 15th World Youth Day, August 19, 2000, no. 5, Holy See, https://www.vatican.va/content/john-paul-ii/en/speeches/2000/jul-sep/documents/hf_jp-ii_spe_20000819_gmg-veglia.html.

5. Fyodor Dostoevsky, *The Idiot*, trans. Constance Garnett (New York: Bantam, 1981), 370.

6. T. S. Eliot, "The Dry Salvages," *Four Quartets*, accessed February 14, 2024, http://www.davidgorman.com/4quartets/3-salvages.htm.

9. Connect Your Story to the Larger Story

1. John Henry Newman, *The Idea of a University Defined and Illustrated* (London: Longmans, Green, 1907), discourse 9, at Newman Reader, National Institute for Newman Studies, https://www.newmanreader.org/works/idea/discourse9.html.

2. Joshua Hren, *How to Read and Write Like a Catholic* (Gastonia, NC: Tan Books, 2021), 34.

3. Alasdair MacIntyre, *After Virtue* (South Bend, IN: University of Notre Dame Press, 2007), 263.

4. St. John Paul II, Apostolic Letter *Mulieris Dignitatem* (*On the Dignity and Vocation of Women*), August 15, 1988, no. 1, Holy See, https://www.vatican.va/content/john-paul-ii/en/apost_letters/1988/documents/hf_jp-ii_apl_19880815_mulieris-dignitatem.html.

Contributors to Stories of a
Well-Read Life

RyAnne Carr is living her dream life on the prairie of North Dakota. She resides in Fargo and spends her days homeschooling her five children. She became passionate about grief and loss after her first child was stillborn and now coaches women on how to see their grief through the eyes of wholeness. She loves growth, Jesus, and encouraging women to be who God made them to be!

Nicki Johnston is a home educator, a Catechesis of the Good Shepherd catechist, an avid reader, and an amateur naturalist. She lives in Kansas with her husband, Graham, and their four young sons.

Teresa Petruccelli received her undergraduate degree from Benedictine College and completed her master's at MidAmerica Nazarene University in Kansas. She currently practices psychotherapy for individuals and couples in St. Paul, Minnesota.

Susan Severson is a wannabe saint, a homeschool slogger, a sometimes-but-wants-to-be-all-the-time writer, and mother to four little rapscallions (with another on the way). Prayers are welcome. She resides in Crosby, Minnesota.

Marcie Stokman is a writer, a speaker, and the president and founder of Well-Read Mom, an organization that accompanies women in the reading of great books and spiritual classics. She is the author of *The Well-Read Mom: Read More. Read Well.*

Stokman earned a bachelor of nursing degree from the University of Nebraska at Kearney and a master of arts degree in psychology from Adler University in Chicago.

Stokman and her husband, Peter, live in Crosby, Minnesota. They have seven children and seventeen grandchildren.

Colleen Hutt is the director of literary evangelization for Well-Read Mom. She has worked as a director of children and adult formation in several parishes in Florida and Wisconsin. She is a catechist, a FOCCUS facilitator for marriage prep, and a retreat leader.

Hutt graduated from the University of Notre Dame with a bachelor of arts degree in liberal studies.

Hutt and her husband, Colin, live in Oconomowoc, Wisconsin. They have five children and one grandchild.

Well~Read Mom

Discover the Well-Read Mom Experience

eclaim Time for Books, Friendship, and Personal Growth

a world bustling with noise and distractions, finding time and space for eaningful conversations and personal growth can be a challenge. Developing d maintaining the ability for deep reading isn't something we can take for anted. Millions of Americans won't read a single book this year. Don't let urself be one of them. We can help!

VHAT WE DO:

/ell-Read Mom accompanies women in the exploration of great books and piritual classics. Our journey is not just about reading; it's about reorienting urselves to what is good, beautiful, and true. Through our carefully selected ading list, we dive deep into the human condition, seeking to uncover the rofound meanings that lie within our daily lives.

UR MATERIALS INCLUDE:

- **Monthly Book Selections:** Carefully chosen to encourage thoughtful reflection and discussion.

- **Discussion Guide:** A beautiful reading companion that provides central ideas, thought-provoking questions, and reflections to deepen your reading experience.

- **Supportive Community:** A network of local groups, each reflecting the unique life experiences of its members, and a broader national community of women who together are reading the same books at the same time.

- **Resources for Growth:** Access to audios, reflections, and materials that complement your reading journey.

- **Summer Magazine:** A beautiful, full-color year-end magazine filled with member reflections, feature articles on reading, motherhood, leisure, and culture, and a preview of the membership year to come!

PLAN THAT WORKS:

nere is no "failing" when you join Well-Read Mom. In Well-Read Mom, you will ot just read more; you will read well. Together, we create a space where truth an be encountered and lives can be transformed. Whether you are a lifelong eader, looking to reignite your love for books, or just starting to develop a reading ractice, Well-Read Mom invites you to join our community.

TAKE CARE OF YOUR HEART
An Invitation from Well-Read Mom to Experience the Renewing Power of Literatur

When a woman joins Well-Read Mom, she is not just purchasing a booklist or product; she is joining and supporting a movement of women who want to read more and read well. We strive to deepen the awareness of meaning in each woman daily life, elevate the cultural conversation, and revitalize the reading of quality literature. Well-Read Mom couldn't exist without the financial support our member provide. We are proud to say that, due to the generosity of our members, no woman is turned away due to financial need.

How to Get Started

Register at **wellreadmom.com**.

Explore our theme for the year and different membership levels.

Find Your Well-Read Mom Community

Join an existing group, start a group, or, if you're not ready for a small-group experience, read along with a friend. Check out our Find Your Community Search Engine to find a group near you or our Leader Resources for more information about starting a group.

Well-Read Mom makes it easy to lead a group. We'll walk with you every step of the way, from inviting the women, hosting an informational meeting, publicizing your group, helping the women get registered, and running a low-stress and meaningful meeting.

Access Our Materials

Once you register, you will have immediate access to our online materials, including current and past booklists, monthly audios, and podcasts. Printed materials will be shipped in late July for the membership year starting in September and within 7-10 days for anyone who joins during the year.

When Well-Read Mom began, we desired to create a place for women not to escape from family life and work but to experience a kind of leisure through friendship and literature so that women could return to their lives with a renewed vision and vigor. By reading books together, we help sustain a tradition of reading, which is a gift to our families and the world. Join us today.

READ MORE. READ WELL.